Moral Vision

Studies in Social, Political, and Legal Philosophy
Series Editor: James P. Sterba, University of Notre Dame

This series analyzes and evaluates critically the major political, social, and legal ideals, institutions, and practices of our time. The analysis may be historical or problem-centered; the evaluation may focus on theoretical underpinnings or practical implications. Among the recent titles in the series are:

The Business of Consumption: Environmental Ethics and the Global Economy
    edited by Laura Westra and Patricia H. Werhane
Child versus Childmaker: Present Duties and Future Persons in Ethics and the Law
    by Melinda A. Roberts
Gewirth: Critical Essays on Action, Rationality, and Community
    edited by Michael Boylan
The Idea of a Political Liberalism: Essays on Rawls
    edited by Victoria Davion and Clark Wolf
Self-Management and the Crisis of Socialism: The Rose in the Fist of the Present
    by Michael W. Howard
Ecofeminist Philosophy: A Western Perspective on What It Is and Why It Matters
    by Karen J. Warren
Controversies in Feminism
    edited by James P. Sterba
Faces of Environmental Racism: Confronting Issues of Global Justice, Second Edition
    edited by Laura Westra and Bill E. Lawson
Theorizing Backlash: Philosophical Reflections on the Resistance to Feminism
    by Anita M. Superson and Ann E. Cudd
Just Ecological Integrity: The Ethics of Maintaining Planetary Life
    edited by Peter Miller and Laura Westra
American Heat: Ethical Problems with the United States' Response to Global Warming
    by Donald A. Brown
Exploitation: What It Is and Why It's Wrong
    by Ruth J. Sample
The Principle of Fairness and Political Obligation, New Edition
    by George Klosko
Moral Vision: How Everyday Life Shapes Ethical Thinking
    by Duane L. Cady

Moral Vision

How Everyday Life Shapes Ethical Thinking

Duane L. Cady

ROWMAN & LITTLEFIELD PUBLISHERS, INC.
Lanham • Boulder • New York • Toronto • Oxford

ROWMAN & LITTLEFIELD PUBLISHERS, INC.

Published in the United States of America
by Rowman & Littlefield Publishers, Inc.
A wholly owned subsidiary of The Rowman & Littlefield Publishing Group, Inc.
4501 Forbes Boulevard, Suite 200, Lanham, Maryland 20706
www.rowmanlittlefield.com

PO Box 317
Oxford
OX2 9RU, UK

British Library Cataloguing-in-Publication Information Available

Library of Congress Cataloging-in-Publication Data

Cady, Duane L.
  Moral vision: how everyday life shapes ethical thinking / Duane L. Cady.
    p. cm. — (Studies in social, political, and legal philosophy)
  Includes index.
  ISBN 0-7425-4493-1 (cloth : alk. paper) — ISBN 0-7425-4494-X (pbk. : alk. paper)
  1. Ethics.   2. Thought and thinking.   3. Judgment (Ethics)   4. Reasoning.
  I. Title.   II. Series.
  BJ1012.C25 2005
  170'.42—dc22   2004024113

Printed in the United States of America

∞™ The paper used in this publication meets the minimum requirements of American
National Standard for Information Sciences—Permanence of Paper for Printed Library
Materials, ANSI/NISO Z39.48-1992.

For four families:
Cadys, Carlsons, Harmelings, and Raymonds

Contents

Preface

[After Dewey's death] a great change came over the face of American philosophy as it used more and more refined logical techniques, squinted its eyes, and peered into smaller and smaller places.

—Morton White

Nearly twenty years ago a senior philosophy major—one of the better students I had known to that point—caught me during office hours and raised a question from which I have never quite recovered. I had something of a reputation on campus for interest in and a bit of activism on various social and political issues. I had been questioning the linkage of eligibility for student financial aid with registration for a possible military draft, encouraging students calling for institutional divestment of endowment holdings in corporations doing business in South Africa under apartheid, supporting a feminist theory course in the Philosophy Department, organizing students to tutor Southeast Asian refugees in English, and so on. My student's question was this: "How do you decide how to spend your time?" When I asked her to clarify and develop the question so that I might understand what she was getting at she said, "Give me your criterion for how you decide when to read philosophy, when to be involved in your various causes and which one, and when to spend time with your family, or when just to relax and do nothing."

All I could do was be honest. I said I didn't have a criterion and that I doubted that one could be developed to account for my behavior. I said I just did the best I could at dealing with the competing demands on my time and conscience; I did what I felt I had to and could do. She smiled broadly and said she thought I should act on reasons rather than on emotions. I said a few more things, none of which adequately answered her question. The conversation collapsed and I knew she left with the smug satisfaction of having made her professor squirm. Of course, her question was not entirely genuine. I had earlier sensed that she did not approve of my active involvement in social and political issues, that somehow such involvement made me less serious, in her mind, as an academic philosopher. So, I had not really disappointed her when I failed to provide a criterion; rather, I had confirmed her suspicions.

Some years later, I had a conversation over lunch during which a similar problem arose, but from the opposite angle. It was with the copy editor for my first book and, although we had worked together by mail and telephone, this was our first meeting in person, occasioned by my travel for a philosophy conference. My book had been out for some months so our luncheon was free of business. An innocent query opened our conversation: I was asked what I had been reading lately. As chance would have it, I had spent the several-hour flight that morning with Richard Rorty's *Contingency, Irony, and Solidarity*. My editor-friend hadn't read it, asked about it, and the conversation turned to morality and reason. Her own moral choices and her concerns for pregnant, unwed teens in Philadelphia led her to find incredible any academic philosopher's suggestion that morality may be without rational foundations; she took the suggestion to encourage wanton disregard among people.

My student found it laughable that I couldn't provide sufficiently rational conditions for my own moral choices. My reading suggested that it may be foolish or naive to expect such conditions. And my editor-friend thought it obvious and necessary that being reasonable is basic to moral behavior. I thought I understood each rationale; I suspected the tensions between them depended on differing conceptions of ethics and rationality, and I have felt a need to attempt reconciling them ever since.

I open with these stories because they turn on the problem I want to explore: What is moral reasoning? Are we being reasonable when we make moral decisions if we cannot supply compelling arguments, criteria, necessary and sufficient conditions, decisive empirical evidence, and the like? It seems that much of contemporary academic philosophy has had the effect of undermining, relativising, deconstructing, and otherwise challenging our claims, including our values, to the point that some scholars talk of the end of philosophy. It has been suggested that philosophy, having undone itself, must be replaced by art, faith, emotion, or literature—*something* outside the traditional confines of argument, evidence, and rationality.

Very broadly speaking, something like inflation has characterized changing conceptions of reason since the Enlightenment, especially in the last fifty years among academic philosophers. What I mean is that what counts as reason has been getting narrower and more precise, following the models of modern science, while at the same time the value of reason has dropped. Earlier and broader understandings of reason, deeper, richer, perhaps more metaphorical, aesthetic, or reflective of life experience not reducible to first-order predicate calculus—understandings like those conveyed by allegory in Plato's dialogues for example—have almost entirely disappeared from mainstream contemporary philosophical accounts of ethical thought. Meanwhile, contemporary critiques of the narrower, more "scientific" understanding of reason have emerged from feminist, antiracist, anticlassist, pragmatic, postmodern, and other perspectives, provoking a pluralistic conversation concerning the nature of philosophy and with it, the nature of ethics. Debate continues on the extent to which the pluralistic turn in ethics is itself philosophic, with twentieth-century Anglo-American analytic philosophy modeling itself after its understanding of modern science and the pluralist critique coming from broader notions of both philosophy and reason.

During my graduate school days in the late 1960s and early 1970s at Brown University, I had a grad-student colleague from Korea, Myung Hyun Lee, who expressed in a memorable seminar session a frustration felt by other graduate students in the department. Struggling to find the right words in English to describe his sense that our analytic methodologies were too narrow to capture the full meanings of the concepts we puzzled over, he blurted out "no vision, no vision." While it wasn't clear how we could reasonably broaden our philosophical examination of the topics at hand given our operative notions of how to do philosophy, I shared his sense of frustration and have carried this memory—and the associated vision metaphor—with me across my career. As clear and precise as our analyses were, it often seemed something was missing and it had to do with a bigger vision than our tools allowed.

Sometimes it is suggested that philosophy cannot do what it has set out to do. Claiming that philosophy can never reconcile tensions between the private (self-fulfillment) and public (community justice) spheres, Richard Rorty recommends a turn away from theory toward narrative in *Contingency, Irony, and Solidarity*. In *After Virtue* Alasdair MacIntyre argues that "we have— very largely if not entirely—lost our comprehension, both theoretical and practical, of morality." Other critics of contemporary philosophical ethics, such as Iris Murdoch, Suzanne Langer, and Martha Nussbaum, take a more expansive view of theory and include aesthetic dimensions such as metaphor and narrative as contributing to theory. I have been exploring these broader understandings of theory within a contemporary pluralistic context, considering recent developments in ethics from diverse racial, class, and gender perspectives, trying to articulate a wider, more inclusive notion of theory and its implications for conceptions of reason and philosophy.

Perhaps philosophy cannot do what it has set out to do unless we conceive of philosophy more broadly; philosophy certainly had been conceived more broadly by most practitioners prior to the reason inflation of the past century. From its earliest forms, philosophical thought has advanced ethical theory as much by the use of description, image, and metaphor as by argumentation modeled after mathematics and empirical science. Below, I try to show that in doing so, philosophers did not abandon either rationality or philosophy for art, literature, faith, or emotion, although there are elements of these in their work.

My general thesis in what follows is that formal reasoning happens within conceptual frameworks but that it cannot prove or provide those frameworks. Metaphor, allegory, parable, narrative, and life experience all reveal constructive visions that frame and guide moral reasoning. While these are not themselves reducible to formal reasoning, neither are they irrational. I am inclined to follow Iris Murdoch's lead in recognizing that there is more to moral reasoning than choice-guiding arguments. Moral differences are not just different choices given the same facts; they are differences of vision. Differences in moral vision can be described by what I will call "life metaphors." They provide conceptual frameworks within which moral reasoning, in the narrower, more formal sense of reason, takes place. For example, if one thinks about one's own life and options from within the metaphor of life as a test, the value implications differ greatly from thinking within the metaphor of life as a journey. From within the test metaphor, moral choices are constrained by notions of being judged, possible future punishment or reward, and so on. Those oriented from within a journey metaphor would more likely make moral choices expressive of valuing exploration, excitement about things new and different, feeling less need for closure, and so on. There are a great many lead metaphors, a wide variety of moral visions, to consider: life as a market, as an organism, a gift, a contest, a machine, an intellectual puzzle, and more, and these are only a few familiar variations within our societal setting; moral visions are considerably more diverse as we reflect on cross-cultural variations.

Reasoning within a life metaphor—or thinking within the framework of one's moral vision—yields decisions reflective of the dominant orientation to life expressed by that metaphor or embraced by that vision. Reason calculates options and guides decisions consistent with the framework of the lead metaphor, but reason in this narrow sense does not get us into or out of life metaphors, does not account for our moral visions, does not prove or provide our conceptual frameworks. In addition to negotiating the interactions—sometimes the collisions—between moral visions, another of the challenges to ethical theory is trying to understand how we get into our moral frameworks, how we identify with and act from within our particular moral visions.

If indeed moral differences are not just different choices given the same facts, but are differences of vision, then it is imperative for ethics to help us get beyond the impasse of recognizing difference. That is, if ethics is to be meaningful in a pluralistic world, we need ways of thinking that can take us beyond both relativism—regarding all moral visions as equals where any choice between them is arbitrary—and dogmatism—regarding one's own moral vision as superior to those of all others and as justifiably imposed on them. The task is to understand how we get our moral visions and then to consider the ethics of negotiating between and among them. My interest is in the extent to which various forms of reason take part in both projects.

Where does our moral vision come from? How is it that we envision the values to which we aspire in our individual and collective behavior and not different ones? Philosophers have had relatively little to say about this explicitly, the tradition largely taking for granted that we reason, reflect, and, to the extent we are reflective agents, choose our values—at least that's the impression one gets from reading traditional philosophy, with its emphasis on premises, argumentation, and conclusions. Philosophers operate as if moral vision is a result of rational decision, and because reason has come to be understood increasingly narrowly and precisely, philosophers have struggled to defend ethics as other than arbitrary. Common sense suggests that moral vision comes from a wide variety of sources. Sometimes it is explicitly taught, but often we form our fundamental moral outlook by growing up within a certain family, absorbing actions and stories of role models both ordinary and famous, or we find affinity with or react against cultural events and patterns around us. We might reflect on imprints of experience, feelings, encounters with moral horror, or acts of generosity and kindness; we might find novels, films, travel, or works of art influential, or perhaps chance encounters or random events provoke value reorientation. Whatever the influences, it seems that argumentation is more likely to follow from than to lead to identification with any particular moral framework. There is plenty of moral disagreement, but it seems that moral visions lead and guide such argumentation, rather than result from it. Few of us are moved to adopt a value perspective based on having accepted premises and arguments leading to that perspective as a conclusion. The arguments we make to defend our value claims rarely are our reasons for embracing them; rather, we trot out reasons and evidence to defend, justify, or even rationalize our moral outlooks, which we hold quite independently of argumentation.

In order to develop this view of moral thought and the elements contributing to moral outlook, I begin by considering important contemporary critiques of traditional conceptions of moral reasoning. A second chapter reviews models of morality that have been prominent in the discipline and examines the role of conceptual frameworks and their normative implications. Chapter 3 goes on to contextualize and to explore the influence of life experience on moral vision, looking at moral horror, moral role models, and experiences with moral import that demand expression even when conventional language is inadequate. In the fourth chapter, I consider aesthetic aspects of moral thought, including the influence of indirect experience, expressions in both fictional and factual narrative accounts, stories, music, film, and visual art, looking at how these influence ethics. Next, the significance of metaphor and particularly what I call life metaphors are considered for their influence on moral reasoning and perspective. A discussion of moral pluralism follows, including considerations of gender, race, class, and nature, opening into a broader consideration of negotiating between moral visions. A closing chapter draws conclusions and examines implications of this effort to reconceive, broaden, and defend moral reasoning. The afterword considers the possibility of moral universality within a context of diversity and relativism.

It must be obvious that this is a very ambitious undertaking. I make no claim to its being exhaustive. The breadth of vision to which this project aspires makes the work suggestive at best. Readers insistent on scholastic, guarded, and algorythmically argumentative prose will be disappointed. Mine is an effort to see a huge set of problems as parts of an interrelated whole, driven by the suspicion that getting the details exactly right throughout would mean losing even a tenuous grasp of the big picture. I examine predominant models of moral thought in the Western philosophical tradition and explore alternatives, but I do not pretend to have it all worked out in any final way. To borrow and extend a conceptual distinction from Thomas Kuhn, I am not trying to do ethics in the normal sense (i.e., work out the implications of functioning within any particular moral paradigm, perspective, or framework); rather, I am calling attention to and reflecting on the significance of moral paradigms themselves. My focus is on the meaning and role of rationality in embracing or rejecting moral paradigms and on negotiating differences, even collisions, between them. Although I consider influences of religion on ethics along with other influences, my approach is philosophical and not at all theological; still, there are significant implications for religious ethics. My central hope in this project is to contribute constructively to an ongoing conversation about forms of reason and pluralism in ethics.

Some of the chapters below are extensions of work done for other occasions. Much of the first chapter was presented at a conference on domination at the University of North Carolina at Charlotte in October 1992. Chapter 3 includes reworkings of a paper on moral horror presented at Villanova University in September 1994, and revisions of a talk on experience and justice presented at McMaster University in 2000. Parts of chapter 6 took their earliest form in my presidential address for a Concerned Philosophers for Peace meeting at the University of Tennessee in Knoxville, October 1991, and other parts are from a talk at the University of Notre Dame in February 1998. The afterword builds on ideas first developed in a presentation on "Diversity, Relativism and Nonviolence," presented at the University of Dayton in 1995, revised and published in *The Acorn: Journal of the Gandhi-King Society* in 1999, and revised again for a presentation at the University of Trier, Germany, in 2004.

Books always reflect relationships and are products of the social contexts from which they come. I am grateful to many for their roles in my thinking, well aware of both their help and my own limitations in attempting to express my thoughts. Many of the ideas in this book have been refined and clarified through conversations in and out of class with many current and former Hamline University students. In particular, I am grateful to Andrew LaZella, a recent graduate, who read the entire manuscript and offered his reactions. I appreciate the seriousness with which Hamline students take philosophy. My gratitude goes also to many current and former colleagues, in particular the regular participants of two faculty organizations at Hamline University: the Lido group, a monthly pedagogical discussion focused on diversity issues in the classroom, and the ongoing Fem Sem, devoted to readings and conversations about feminism. Colleen Bell, Jim Bonilla, and Veena Deo have been especially helpful. Several close friends encouraged and supported this work, often when they least suspected as much. I have in mind Sam Imbo, Julie Raulli, Hugh Stephenson, Rick Werner, and Peter Woolrich. Michael Price, long-time friend, sculptor, and colleague shared many conversations on ethics and aesthetics with me, challenging and encouraging my work; I've missed Mike and our conversations since his death in April 2001.

I have always taken my teachers more seriously than I have given them reason to believe. My undergraduate professors at Hamline University opened a world of ideas to a blue-collar kid who had no idea where such exposure might lead; one in particular, Joseph N. Uemura, prodded and challenged me as no one had before (and as few have since). My graduate professors at Brown University modeled scholarship and teaching for me while providing an important balance between freedom and structure. I'm especially grateful for having studied with Rod Chisholm and Bill Lenz. My Hamline University colleagues, Tom Atchison, Nancy Holland, Sam Imbo, Stephen Kellert, and David Owen (now of the University of Louisville), as well as emeritus colleagues Huston Smith and Joseph Uemura, have given support and criticism, respecting if not always agreeing with what I have been doing professionally. Their direct and indirect comments on this work, particularly suggestions from Nancy, Sam, and Stephen, helped me immeasurably. Claude Brew of Gustavus Adolphus

College read the whole manuscript, providing important stylistic advice. Deane Curtin, also of Gustavus, Barry Gan of St. Bonaventure University, Sara Ruddick of Eugene Lang College, New School for Social Research, Jim Sterba of the University of Notre Dame, Rick Werner of Hamilton College, and Karen Warren of Macalester College all have been generous with their encouragement, making valuable suggestions. I am honored to have all these colleagues as friends.

Generations of the four families to whom this book is dedicated—Cadys, Carlsons, Harmelings, and Raymonds—have provided a moral context within which I have been nurtured, criticized, and sustained. The moral visions and metaphors of my grandparents and parents loom large behind my words, often in harmony, occasionally in dissonance, always influencing. The families into which I married adopted me as a son and grandson, brother, nephew, and uncle, with grace and generosity. Their influence on my thinking was inescapable.

I appreciate the support of my home institution, Hamline University, for a sabbatical leave for the academic year 2001–2002. While this set of issues has been on my mind for more than a decade, and many shorter papers and presentations written over the years have been taken apart and revised into parts of this book, I could not have completed a unified manuscript without a full year free from teaching and other university obligations. The confidence of those colleagues who reviewed and endorsed my sabbatical proposal—Diane Clayton, Cynthia Cone, Garvin Davenport, Kim Guenther, Ted Hodapp, Stephen Kellert, Tamara Root, Bill Wallace, and Dwight Watson—has been more important than they know. I am grateful for the interest and encouragement of Eve DeVaro Fowler, Acquisitions Editor at Rowman & Littlefield, and to her reviewers and copy editors for valuable advice and assistance.

Finally, I must express thanks to my immediate family—spouse Sandy, daughter Annie, son Ton, and daughter-in-law Karis. They are ongoing sources of joy, love, and honesty, believing in what I was trying to do even when I had my doubts, and calling my views into question when I took myself too seriously. I have learned more from them than can be repaid.

D.L.C.
St. Paul, Minnesota

Chapter One

Ethics and Rationality

The intellectual public is waiting to hear from art what it has not heard
from Theology, Philosophy, Social Theory and what it cannot hear from
pure science: a broader, fuller, more coherent, more comprehensive account of what we human beings are, who we are and what this life is for.
If writers do not come to the center it will not be because the center is pre-
empted. It is not.

—Saul Bellow

Philosophy is not what it used to be. More than 2,000 years ago, Aristotle suggested that it was a sense of wonder that first moved humans to philosophize.
For centuries, the subject matter evolved, driven by wonder, but increasingly
practiced in service to the church or other institutions. By the late eighteenth
century, the field had come to be more and more technical, still bearing the
mark of wonder, yet less conspicuously so. Perhaps due to the rise of the
modern university or to the development of modern science or both, by the
mid-twentieth century, philosophy, like most academic disciplines, had become highly specialized, most practitioners had been trained as technical experts, and the discipline was increasingly a professional vocation. An expo-
nential expansion of scholarship seemed to parallel the diminishing role of
wonder in the work of philosophers. Nonetheless, students in the field—
especially the young—continued, as always, to be drawn to philosophy out of
a sense of wonder.

The astounding successes of natural science prompted practitioners of virtually every discipline in the Western intellectual tradition to revise methodologies, adopting increasingly mathematical and empirical elements in their
epistemologies. The logical positivist criterion of meaning, the notion that
statements are meaningful only if they are either empirically verifiable or

1

significant in virtue of the definitions of the terms in which they are expressed, has left an indelible mark on Western philosophy. While few philosophers embrace positivism in its pure form, Anglo-American philosophy has been transformed by increased expectations for technical precision, empirical test, logical analysis, and a general tendency to model the reasoning patterns of science and mathematics.

Modeling philosophy after science is nothing new, nor has it been without its ironies. Historically, every period of scientific progress has been followed by a flurry of philosophical productivity as scientific forms of reason are adapted to philosophic problems. Nonetheless, some of the most influential philosophers in the Western intellectual tradition might not be taken very seriously today if they were held to contemporary standards of reason. Dialogues like those of Plato or meditations like those of Descartes would be unlikely to satisfy current publication guidelines. My point is not the truism that times have changed nor that much is known today that could not have been known decades or centuries ago; such can be said about any academic discipline. My point is that philosophical insight seems irreducible to any narrow criterion, regardless of how successful that criterion may be in various fields. Philosophy, by its nature, reaches beneath, behind, and beyond the confines of even its own criteria. Such efforts are not always successful, but they are characteristic of the intellectual enterprise of philosophy.

Resistance to limitations on the scope of philosophy is especially evident regarding questions and issues concerning values. Ethics, aesthetics, and social and political philosophy all defy easy subsumption under science-inspired epistemological restrictions. Science has not had much success understanding values, and great philosophic contributions in ethics, aesthetics, and social and political theory are more likely to be ancient, medieval, or modern than contemporary. Some regard the "lack of progress" in values, by comparison with scientific progress, as evidence for the irrationality of values. Others call for increased scientific investigation of value issues. Still others suggest that progress is a problematic concept not only regarding values but for science as well. It is worth noting that Aristotle counseled his students to remember that disciplines differ due to differing natures of the objects of their studies and that "the educated person seeks exactness in each area to the extent that the nature of the subject allows," recognizing that it is reasonable to expect proof in some areas but to look for no more than persuasion in others.[1]

The ordinary understanding of science as a linear, cumulative, and steadily growing body of timeless and universal objective knowledge persists despite powerful challenges from historians and theorists of science. Thomas Kuhn provided an early instance of what has come to be an avalanche of critiques and alternate visions of science with *The Structure of Scientific Revolutions* in 1962. For Kuhn, even science cannot meet the standards of science as it is characterized in popular textbooks because actual scientific practices belie the characterization. Science turns out to be a historically bound human activity explorative of experience and nature rather than a finished set of achievements descriptive of the way things actually are. If science itself falls short of the ordinary conception of scientific rigor, why would anyone expect philosophy, especially ethics, to meet such narrow standards of rationality?

Nonetheless, in the Western intellectual tradition, philosophical ethics has been characterized by an emphasis on argument, abstract theory, formal reasoning, and foundation principles. All of these have been taken to be largely distinct from emotional, aesthetic, narrative, and creative considerations. Recent criticisms of traditional philosophical ethics, from antiracist, feminist, pragmatic, deconstructive, anticlassist, environmental, postmodern, and other perspectives have provoked pluralistic conversations concerning the nature of philosophy. These conversations have, in turn, transformed ethics. Debate continues on the extent to which the pluralistic turn in ethics is philosophic and on the meaning and role of reason in morality.

Some contemporary critics suggest that philosophy cannot do what it has set out to do. For example, in *Contingency, Irony, and Solidarity*, Richard Rorty explores what he takes to be a fundamental tension in Western thought, namely, the tension between human needs for private self fulfillment on the one hand and for community on the other. Rorty asserts that there is no way for philosophy, or any other theoretical discipline, to bring "self-creation and justice, private perfection and human solidarity" under one comprehensive theory. He urges philosophers to accept that we cannot synthesize personal autonomy with justice and he recommends that we drop the demand for reasoned accounts attempting to do so. Rorty regards the claims to private fulfillment and to human solidarity as equally valid but insists that they are "forever incommensurable." He sees the language of self-creation as private and unsuited to argument whereas the language of justice is public and argumentative. Having precluded traditional grounds for resolving conceptual conflict, Rorty turns against theory and toward narrative. The bulk of his book is devoted to the notion that what philosophers have taken to be reasoning has actually been description and redescription, an echo of his *Philosophy and the Mirror of Nature*. He turns to novelists for guidance toward freedom and against cruelty because he regards them to be unlike philosophers in their honesty: they do not pretend to reveal reality; rather, they provide interesting and useful metaphors.[2]

Rorty has a conception of reason that he has come to believe philosophy cannot achieve. It seems to me to be the same notion of reason that has been predominant for the past few generations of practitioners in the Western philosophical tradition, an idea of reason modeled after the image of textbook natural science, where arguments and evidence compel thinkers to objective conclusions about reality itself. Rorty is not alone; his work is exemplary of an important and influential development in contemporary philosophy, giving rise to renewed interest in pragmatism. Distanced from more traditional ethical thought by eschewing metaphysics, neopragmatism has found a significant following in recent years.

Another important critique of traditional Western ethics has come from Alasdair MacIntyre. *After Virtue* is rightly considered one of the most important books in twentieth-century ethics. In it, MacIntyre argues that the only way to regain a rationally and morally defensible standpoint from which to judge and to act requires us to reject the *ethos* of our distinctively modern world because we have no rational way of securing moral agreement. Ethical disputes are quickly reduced to assertion and counter-assertion; without good reasons, we are stuck with the arbitrariness of nonrational decisions. For MacIntyre, we have lost the contexts that, in the past, gave meaning to moral language; consequently, we are left talking and acting as if emotivism were true, as if our moral talk only expresses our feelings, nothing more. The modern concept of a human life, the individual freed from social bonds and hierarchical authority, leaves us with bureaucracy and individualism, but without rational grounds for morality. Ancient and medieval cultural beliefs and practices of our ancestors gave them moral meaning, but modernity rejected those foundations so our moral claims go without meaning.[3]

Both Rorty and MacIntyre critique contemporary moral philosophy by identifying failures of reason. Both note the irony of modernity reasoning its way to undermine reason, and both suggest we look outside of reason to save moral meaning. While MacIntyre looks to cultural beliefs and practices like those rejected by modernity, Rorty turns to narrative.

In his novel *Immortality*, Milan Kundera introduces the notion of imagology while discussing the ways political propaganda is used to manipulate the values of citizens:

> Are you objecting that advertising and propaganda cannot be compared, because one serves commerce and the other ideology? You understand nothing. Some one hundred years ago in Russia, persecuted Marxists began to gather secretly in small circles in order to study Marx's manifesto; they simplified the contents of this simple ideology in order to disseminate it to other circles, whose members, simplifying further and further this simplification of the simple, kept passing it on and on, so that when Marxism became known and powerful on the whole planet, all that was left of it was a collection of six or seven slogans so poorly linked that it can hardly be called an ideology. And precisely because the

remnants of Marx no longer form any *logical* system of *ideas*, but only a series of suggestive images and slogans (a smiling worker with a hammer, black, white and yellow men fraternally holding hands, the dove of peace rising to the sky, and so on), we can rightfully talk of a gradual, general, planetary transformation of ideology into imagology.[4]

I am interested in this passage from Kundera for several reasons. First, it fits with Rorty's suggestion that moral views are less the product of reasoning and more the result of an image, a slogan, a metaphor. On the other hand, I am interested in this passage because it seems quite philosophic; Kundera challenges the dominant notion of ideology as accounting for social values and offers the more cynical yet quite serious suggestion of capturing and influencing public opinion with simplifications of the simple, what he calls imagology. In doing so, Kundera is reasoning philosophically. He is making an argument, probing for reasons behind or beneath the given, appealing to the evidence of our experience after reflective consideration, and asking us (as did Plato, Hobbes, Arendt, and every other social theorist) whether the given account rings true. Still further, I am interested in Kundera's thinking on this issue because Kundera is a novelist, thereby free of the pretense Rorty attributes to philosophers (and others practicing theoretical disciplines). Yet it seems to me that Kundera deals in reasons and ideas, not just in narrative and redescription. I imagine that Rorty might enjoy the irony of my appeal to Kundera, a novelist, to defend theory against Rorty's recommendation that we abandon theory for narrative.

"Theory" comes from the Greek *theoria*, "a viewing, looking at, beholding, observing"; when said of the mind, it refers to "a contemplation, a reflection."[5] *Theoria* is a kind of seeing, whether of the external, physical sort, or of the reflective, intellectual sort. The shared linguistic root with "theater" reflects both sorts of seeing, visual and rational, sight and insight.

Etymologically, Rorty makes an odd turn when he counsels us to join his move away from theory and toward narrative. He says that philosophy (and other theoretical disciplines) offer only description and redescription, giving us nothing more than another way of looking at an issue. In a way he is right; this is what philosophy—theory generally—has always done. Consider the images, allegories, parables, and metaphors that help us focus on the ideas of Plato: the ring of Gyges; the allegory of the metals; the parable of the cave; the metaphor of Socrates as a midwife; the laws coming to Socrates in a dream; the myth of Er; the image of weaving; the analogy of the aviary; the ship of state; the soul as charioteer; the metaphor of harmony in the soul; the simile of the sun; and the constant analogies to goatherds, cobblers, physicians, bakers, and on and on. And these are only a few of the images, and only from Plato. It seems that theory—offering ways to see—is, or at least can be, philosophic, if the contemplation and resulting reflection call the given into question and deepen our understanding. Apparently, Rorty thinks we expect theory to deliver formal or empirical proof of absolute reality, and he is out to disabuse us of these expectations. But surely we are not surprised; formal proofs happen within theories, not outside of them, and philosophical claims about reality are more aspirations than finished accomplishments. Theories give us ways of seeing the issues we struggle with, and we choose among them as we take them to be more or less helpful, more or less accurate in accounting for our experience. Formal proof helps us work out the details, thoroughly and consistently, within a given theoretical frame. With enough inconsistency of detail, we may alter a theory or even abandon it for another. But we do not choose to adopt a theory because we are forced to the choice by formal reasoning.

This is not to say that all narrative is theoretical. Many stories are only stories and do not have reflections, criticism, foundation examination, and deepening understanding of basic issues as their purpose. This is why we think of poets, novelists, and playwrights as more or less philosophical (some so much less so than others as to be thought not at all philosophic, and others so much more so that we hardly know how to distinguish them from philosophers). The point is that narrative may serve theory, and, to the extent that it does so, it is philosophic; there is no need to choose between narrative and theory.

Something similar might be said regarding MacIntyre's critique. The reason-rug can be pulled out from under moral talk if reason is characterized narrowly enough, but must it be so characterized? Requiring specific cultural beliefs and practices as foundational for moral meaning does lead to denying meaning where those foundations are absent. But are our moral conversations merely the emotive exchanges MacIntyre suggests? Perhaps not. We certainly intend to mean more than simply expressing irrational emotive preferences when we make moral judgments. Might reason be a larger notion than the one MacIntyre critiques?

It seems pretty clear that moral reasoning is not formal proof construction nor is it reducible to typical patterns of quasi-scientific reasoning; expecting it to be either may be, paraphrasing Aristotle, looking for more precision—or the wrong kind of precision—than that to which the subject matter admits. The fact that moral thought involves metaphors and is not algorithmic does not reduce it to mere description and redescription or to irrational emotive expression. The function of theory is to provide ways of seeing, to give us insight. Moral reasoning happens when one's outlook takes a moral perspective that guides reflection on judgment, choice, and decision. This is why being moral is more than doing certain things and refraining from doing others; being moral involves grasping concepts, accepting specific moral norms, using them as guides, recognizing situations as relevant to the moral norms, and being moved to act accordingly out of deference to them as moral guides. All of this involves reasoning beyond description and redescription. Moral theory involves reflection, criticism, and comparison of various moral perspectives based on their implications, consistency, and fit with our broader vision of our world. Moral reasoning is not likely to be reduced to a calculus, but neither does it collapse into narrative or mere emotional expression beyond reason and theory.

Rorty and MacIntyre both criticize contemporary ethical theory by pointing to the failings of reason, and both look outside of reason to restore moral meaning. But other important critics of contemporary ethical theory, recognizing similar problems, turn instead to a broader conception of reason. Here, I am especially interested in suggestions from Iris Murdoch, Susanne Langer, Martha Nussbaum, and Paul Gilroy.

In "Vision, Choice and Morality," Iris Murdoch recognizes that there is more to moral reasoning than what she calls "choice-guiding arguments." As she sees it, ethical theory cannot be reduced to the search for a mechanism into which we can plug moral puzzles and out of which will pop answers. In our moral apprehensions and assessments, we consider not only "solutions to specifiable practical problems, we consider something more elusive which may be called their total vision of life." In this view, "moral differences look less like differences of choice, given the same facts, and more like differences of vision . . . more like a total difference of *Gestalt*."[6] A well-known novelist as well as a philosopher, Murdoch used her considerable writing skills to explore the subtleties and complexities of these differences of life-vision, offering richly textured and nuanced characterizations of moral dilemmas.

Susanne Langer was another early critic of the then predominant approach to understanding the meaning of value claims. With *Philosophy in a New Key*, Langer offers a formidable challenge to the narrowly restrictive notions of reason and meaning operating in the shadow of logical positivism. While acknowledging that modern theory of knowledge represented the best philosophical work of her time, she went on to add that "'knowledge' is not synonymous with 'human mentality,'" noting that "philosophical thought moves typically from a first, inadequate, but ardent apprehension of some novel idea, figuratively expressed, to more and more precise comprehension, until language catches up to logical insight." For Langer, new concepts always make their initial appearance in metaphorical statements. Her title, *Philosophy in a New Key*, underscores this notion as it subtly challenges the restrictive logical positivist criterion of meaning by holding up the meaningfulness of music. Her interest is in all intellectual activity, taking the study of symbol and meaning as a starting point in philosophy and not excluding nondiscursive symbolisms like myth, ritual, and the arts.[7]

Recognizing that speech is a natural outcome of one kind of human symbolic process, Langer is open to thinking about others. She does not reduce humanity to a least common denominator by insisting that every human capacity must somehow serve the survival of the species; rather, she takes meaning seriously as something more than a means to an end. A great deal of meaning is reducible to signs functioning as signals, that is, as proxies for their referent objects. Much conventional use of language works this way, as do traffic lights and musical notation. But symbols are not stand-ins for their objects, they are vehicles for the conception of objects; "it is the conceptions, not the things, that symbols directly 'mean.'" Understanding symbols involves an unconscious, spontaneous process of abstraction, which we do all the time. And, for Langer, "abstractive seeing is the foundation of our rationality."[8] Verbal symbolization is discursiveness. "So long as we admit only discursive symbolism as a bearer of ideas, 'thought' in this restricted sense must be regarded as our only intellectual activity." Langer goes on to say that "in our experience there are things which do not fit the grammatical scheme of expression. But they are not necessarily blind, inconceivable, mystical affairs; they are simply matters which require to be conceived through some symbolic schema other than discursive language."[9]

Feeling and Form is Langer's theory of art developed from *Philosophy in a New Key*. "The basic concept is the articulate but nondiscursive form having import without conventional reference, and therefore presenting itself not as a symbol in the ordinary sense, but as a 'significant form,' in which the factor of significance is not logically discriminated but is felt as a quality rather than recognized as a function."[10] Langer extends her reach beyond the positivist restrictions on meaning predominant in her day, making an important contribution to aesthetics that continues to reward her readers. Unfortunately, few thinkers have played philosophy in the new key; perhaps Will Durant was onto something when he quipped, in the preface to *The Story of Philosophy*, that epistemology had kidnapped the profession and well-nigh ruined it.

How might nondiscursive, articulate form contribute to our ethical thinking? Consider the powerful and complex image constituting Picasso's *Guernica*, the wall-sized black, white, and gray painting that depicts simple women, children, and domestic animals under siege. While a range of interpretations is possible for this canvas, nonetheless it conveys the horror, chaos, suffering, death, and destruction of war and its impact on ordinary people to every serious viewer. Clearly, the painting's import is not a formal logical derivation, nor is it translatable into conventional language; rather, the significance is felt as a quality. It contributes to our ethical thinking by confronting us with an image of war so powerful that our reaction may be visceral, and in doing so it provokes us to think again about war, about the implications of war for ordinary people's lives, and about our own values. If we engage the image seriously, we find ourselves somehow uncomfortable, challenged, even threatened, not due to thought based on textbook conceptions of scientific reasoning but due to reflections on our sense of who we are, how we are to interact with others, and what we are to value. These will involve not just a calculative function of thinking or a criterion for empirical verification, but a larger vision of life and our place in it. A utilitarian might be challenged to consider not whether this or that war or battle contributes to the greater good for the greater number of beings in sentient creation, but whether calculations like these make sense in the face of such horror. A Kantian might be challenged not so much to demonstrate the consistency or inconsistency of willing to kill in war but to wonder whether the categorical imperative helps us understand how to live in a world where war is common. Nondiscursive, articulate forms can prompt deep and persistent moral thinking that goes not just to the heart of our values, but to the heart of the very frameworks we use for assigning and comparing values.

Clearly, Iris Murdoch and Susanne Langer resisted and defied the restrictions on philosophy that prevailed in the 1940s and 1950s. With *Love's Knowledge*, Martha Nussbaum provides a more recent case for stretching the boundaries. Describing her own experience as a graduate student at Harvard in the late 1960s and early 1970s, she cites a focus on the dominant positions in ethics, when Kantianism and utilitarianism "were taken to divide the field more-or-less exhaustively." Disappointment that "the ethical contribution of literary works was not taken to be a part of Greek ethical thought as such" no doubt helped motivate *The Fragility of Goodness*, Nussbaum's landmark study of ancient Greek tragedians and philosophers, in which she demonstrates the necessity of reintegrating literary texts then almost entirely segregated from ethics scholarship. She takes seriously the ancient goal of ethical inquiry: to improve us, to move us closer to leading good lives. Noting that the prevailing conventional style of Anglo-American philosophic prose was "scientific, abstract, hygienically pallid . . . a kind of all-purpose solvent in which philosophical issues of any kind at all could be efficiently disentangled, any and all conclusions neatly disengaged," Nussbaum attributed it to "the long-standing fascination of Western philosophers with the methods and the style of natural science, which have at many times in history seemed to embody the only sort of rigor and precision worth cultivating, the only norm of rationality worth emulating."[11]

Because she believes that it is a mistake to take the supposed method and style of scientific investigation and apply them to a sphere of life that may demand a different norm of rationality, Nussbaum prefers to begin, like Plato and Aristotle, with the fundamental question of ethics: how should one live? The trick is starting without stacking the deck to favor a particular answer. If we begin by asking "What is my moral duty?" or "What must I do to bring about the greatest good for the greatest number of sentient beings?" the questions themselves rest on assumptions—better, presumptions—that will preclude some answers and encourage others. Nussbaum is careful to acknowledge that there is no perfectly neutral beginning point but notes that this does not mean that all beginnings are equal, arbitrary, or irrational. Some are better than others if those taking them are self-critical and committed to the serious investigation of alternative positions.[12]

In my own life I have found that few if any of us hold consistently to any one ethical theory as we sort through the moral challenges we face. Sometimes we are preoccupied with thinking through our options to determine their likely consequences. Sometimes we are intent on acting with respect to a specific rule regardless of the outcome. Sometimes we are caught up in cross-examining ourselves about the traits of character we most want to manifest in our behavior. Sometimes we notice ourselves acting more-or-less spontaneously out of compassion for another, or out of deference to social norms. And sometimes we are caught in a combination of these concerns, and with other concerns as well. To the extent we are reflective, we may think about how to bring our moral lives under some sort of theoretical frame, categorize our actions under various headings, describe our patterns of behavior to ourselves in general terms, or try in some other way to bring together our disparate acts into a unified moral vision. Always the issue is the fit between what we value and what we do; often, our life experiences give us reason to question what we value even as our values give us reason to question our actions.

The beauty of beginning with a big question like "How are we to live?" is that it leaves open what may count as an appropriate answer and it leaves open what may count as reasons in support of answers. It does not, Nussbaum tells us, "assume that there is, among the many ends and activities that human beings cherish and pursue, some one domain, the domain of moral value, that is of special importance and dignity, apart from the rest of life. Nor does it assume, as do utility theorists, that there is a more or less unitary something that a good agent can be seen as maximizing in every act of choice." The goal of morality is not some sort of correspondence between theory and an objective reality; rather, the goal is "for the best overall fit between a view and what is deepest in human lives." This fit involves coherence among our judgments, feelings, perceptions, and principles, all taken together as a whole.[13] There is no single criterion, no set of necessary and sufficient conditions, no formula from which we can derive a good life. Rather, we search for and struggle to construct answers to the question, "How are we to live?" and we test our answers and those of others against our lives in the deepest and fullest sense.

In *Love's Knowledge*, Nussbaum goes on to make the case for the necessity of including literary works in our moral theorizing, in part by demonstrating the value she has found in particular literary texts and their contributions to moral understanding. Like Rorty, she sees value in turning to narrative for help with our moral lives, but unlike him, she opts for inclusion of the literary within theory where appropriate, rather than for a turn away from theory. In this regard, Nussbaum joins Murdoch and Langer in resisting the mainstream stylistic and methodological conventions of Anglo-American philosophy in the twentieth century. All of them challenge the dominant approach as incomplete and look to various aspects of our lives for meaning beyond the narrow confines of reason patterned after conventional science and logic.

Another challenge to conventional philosophical ethics has come, increasingly since the 1960s, from a wide variety of sources questioning mainstream theory on behalf of underrepresented groups: people of color, women, working-class people, and others. An important example is Paul Gilroy's *The Black Atlantic*, a rethinking of modernity through the history of the experiences of the African diaspora in the Western hemisphere. Gilroy asks us to set aside categories of dominant culture, of modernity, because people of color and the poor are often invisible to the modern world. Modern morality disintegrates as the oldest democracy is founded on a document declaring "these truths to be self-evident, that all Men are created equal, that they are endowed by their Creator with certain unalienable Rights, that among these are Life, Liberty, and the Pursuit of Happiness."[14] People of color and women were excluded from full and equal citizenship by the U.S. founders. If the exclusion was not deliberate, then inclusion must not have occurred to them. Either way, the original arrangement locates power and privilege with a relative few and the universal Enlightenment principles are neither universal nor enlightened as they play out in lived experience. "The politics of fulfillment practiced by the descendants of slaves demands . . . that bourgeois civil society live up to the promises of its own rhetoric."[15] Gilroy asks us to consider black Atlantic cultural expression as a counterculture, "as a philosophical discourse which refuses the modern, occidental separation of ethics and aesthetics, culture and politics." He believes that the modern tradition "lost its exclusive claim to rationality partly through the way that slavery became internal to western civilization and through the obvious complicity which both plantation slavery and colonial regimes revealed between rationality and the practice of racial terror."[16] Sadly, traditional ethical theory rarely acknowledges such complicity; some things remain invisible.

Gilroy is an especially important example of the pluralistic critique of modern ethical thought, not only because he complicates our reconsideration of ethical theory with race, gender, and class issues, but also because he engages aspects of culture explicitly excluded from conventional philosophical ethics and sees them as central to the moral life of the counterculture. Consistent with but not dependent on Susanne Langer's interest in music as significant yet nondiscursive articulate form, Gilroy argues that black musical expression has helped reproduce a distinctive counterculture of modernity. In addition, "by posing the world as it is against the world as the racially subordinated would like it to be, this musical culture supplies a great deal of the courage required to go on living in the present." Citing Adorno's reflections on European artistic expression following the holocaust, Gilroy suggests that for descendants of slaves as well, artistic expression "becomes the means toward both individual self-fashioning and communal liberation."[17] Certainly such expression is relevant to moral theory.

Mainstream philosophy since the Enlightenment has valued progress as involving the steady improvement of society through liberated reason. But the universal claims of this Enlightenment-inspired rational progress contrast markedly with history. The intimate association of modernity with slavery is somehow absent from accounts of modernity, prompting not only a version of double consciousness in the dominant culture, so the obvious can remain invisible, but also prompting a "refusal to subordinate the particularity of the slave experience to the totalizing power of universal reason," leading to an aesthetics of personalism where "the particular can wear the mantle of truth and reason as readily as the universal." Just as slave narratives shatter the elegant universality of democratic principles, exposing the gulf between founding documents and lived experience, artistic expressions from people of color, the poor, and the disfranchised within what is called the Third World all may provide insight into ethics rarely available from mainstream philosophy. Gilroy suggests that hope for a broader, more inclusive and complete ethics rests in part on making room within our conceptions of ethics and reason for a liberatory aesthetic that is "anti- or even pre-discursive."[18] Again, the narrow concept of reason in ethics is challenged.

Etymologically, "ethics" comes from a context considerably broader than that of conventional notions of reason. The word derives from the ancient Greek *ethos*, which means habit or custom. Asking "How are we to live?" and noting that the goal is action and not knowledge, Aristotle, in his *Nicomachean Ethics*, tells us "we need to have been brought up in fine habits [*ethos*] if we are to be adequate students of what is fine and just. . . . [I]f we have this fine upbringing, we have the origins to begin from."[19] Clearly, Aristotle understood that ethical theory does not happen in a vacuum; there is no neutral starting point. Each of us brings our selves, our lives, our patterns of behavior to our ethical reflections. Perhaps it was gratitude for the home life in which he was raised—and where his character, his behavior pattern, was formed—that led Aristotle to name this work for his father, Nicomachus. Aristotle goes on to complete the etymology of ethics for us: "Virtue of character results from habit; hence its name "ethical," slightly varied from *ethos*."[20] MacIntyre reminds us that Cicero invented the word *moralis* to translate the Greek word *ethikos* because there was no corresponding word in Latin. So, our "moral" stands to "moré" as ethical stands to "ethos," the hard consonants in each case indicating a variation from habit, custom, pattern of behavior, to right habit, correct pattern of behavior, excellence of character. Etymologically, the difference between ethics and morals rests on the language of derivation, Greek or Latin. Both words refer to the same thing.

"Reason" comes from Old French, *raison*, which itself derived from Latin, *rationis*, in turn deriving from *ratus*, past participle of *reri*, to think. Through its long history, "reason" has come to mean, as a noun, a motive, explanation or defense of an action or a belief; as a verb it means to think carefully and logically, to use good judgment. Being reasonable can mean anything from being of sound mind (i.e., not insane) to being governed by a specific form or criterion of what is acceptable in the way of explanation or defense of actions and beliefs in a given situation. Clearly, what is acceptable varies with the context of reasoning. Standards of acceptability differ within as well as between areas of action and belief. Aristotle opens his ethical theorizing by reminding readers that reasonable people look for the standards of reason to fit the subject. What is reasonable for a poet at work writing poetry may or may not contribute to the effectiveness of a mathematician constructing a formal proof, or a neurosurgeon in surgery, and vice versa. Nonetheless, practitioners within given areas of action or belief can and do disagree over what constitutes the standards of reason for those areas.

Our problem is figuring out what counts as reason in ethics. What we have seen from Aristotle, and what we have seen from a sampling of critics of contemporary ethical theory above, indicate that regarding ethics, there is considerable disagreement over what should be accepted in the way of explanation or defense of actions or beliefs, that is, over what constitute legitimate forms of reason. We have seen everything from fairly narrow academic conventions of reason modeled after textbook science to very broad notions including emotional, aesthetic, cross-cultural, and experiential contributions for explaining and defending behavior and opinions. I do not pretend to settle this matter in any final way here. In what follows, I explore the boundaries of the dominant philosophic tradition and consider forms of reason at the edges of those boundaries. Taking encouragement from the work of Iris Murdoch, Susanne Langer, Martha Nussbaum, Paul Gilroy, and many others, and formed by the contexts within which I have been steeped, I attempt to help widen what counts as reason in ethics.

NOTES

1. Aristotle, *Nicomachean Ethics* (1094b), 24–27.

2. Rorty, Richard, *Contingency, Irony, and Solidarity* (New York: Cambridge University Press, 1989), xiii–xvi.

3. MacIntyre, Alasdair, *After Virtue* (Notre Dame, IN: University of Notre Dame Press, 1981), x, 8–34.

4. Kundera, Milan, *Immortality* (New York: Grove Press, 1991), 113–14.

5. Liddell, Henry George, and Robert Scott, *Greek-English Lexicon* (Oxford, UK: Oxford University Press, 1871, 1976), 317.

6. Murdoch, Iris, "Vision and Choice in Morality," Proceedings of the Aristotelian Society, 1956, in *Christian Ethics and Contemporary Philosophy*, ed. Ian Ramsey (New York: Macmillan, 1966), 40–41.

7. Langer, Susanne, *Philosophy in a New Key* (Cambridge, MA: Harvard University Press, 1942), ix–xiv.

8. Langer, *Philosophy in a New Key*, 61, 72.

9. Langer, *Philosophy in a New Key*, 88.

10. Langer, Susanne, *Feeling and Form* (New York: Charles Scribner's Sons, 1953), 32.

11. Nussbaum, Martha, *Love's Knowledge* (New York: Oxford University Press, 1990), 13–14, 19.

12. Nussbaum, *Love's Knowledge*, 19–20, 24–25.

13. Nussbaum, *Love's Knowledge*, 25–26.

14. The Declaration of Independence, United States of America.

15. Gilroy, Paul, *The Black Atlantic: Modernity and Double Consciousness* (Cambridge, MA: Harvard University Press, 1993), 37.

16. Gilroy, *Black Atlantic*, 38–39.

17. Gilroy, *Black Atlantic*, 36, 40.

18. Gilroy, *Black Atlantic*, 69, 71.

19. Aristotle, *Nicomachean Ethics* (1095b), 4–9.

20. Aristotle, *Nicomachean Ethics* (1103a), 16–17.

Chapter Two

Moral Frameworks

[I]ntelligence is a slippery customer; if one door is closed to it, it finds or even breaks another entrance to the world. If one symbolism is inadequate, it seizes another; there is no eternal decree over its means and methods. So I will go with the logisticians and linguists as far as they like, but I do not promise to go no further. For there is an unexplored possibility of genuine semantic beyond the limits of discursive language.

—Susanne Langer

Traditional ethical theories are attempts to organize claims about how we ought to live. They tend to focus on capturing both the meaning and standards of the good life, showing how moral assertions follow from comprehensive principles. Philosophers talk about ethical theory in two ways. One refers to normative content, the moral view of right and wrong expressed in an ethical position. For example, "stealing is wrong" is a moral claim for which a normative ethical theory would provide explanation and justification. "Ethical theory" can also refer to a level of abstraction once removed from moral claims and their justifications; this second reference to ethical theory can be thought of as "talk about moral talk," as distinct from moral talk itself. Rather than explaining and justifying normative moral claims, ethical theorists in this second sense think and talk about the characteristics of ethical theories in the first sense; rather than making claims about right and wrong, they make claims about ethical theories. Sometimes this second sort of ethical theory is called "meta-ethics," *meta* being Greek for after or beyond.

There have been a great many ethical theorists in the Western intellectual tradition, the vast majority doing ethical theory in the first sense noted above. Increasingly over the past century philosophers think and talk about ethics in both senses, normative and meta-ethical. Because this distinction is a relatively recent development in the long history of philosophy, both aspects of ethical theory are often intertangled in pre-twentieth-century thought. In discussing moral frameworks here, emphasis is on meta-ethics, yet normative content is described to identify the views in question. The point is to recognize that philosophers tend to talk and think about ethics by reference to relatively few distinct approaches. Here, the *approaches* are the focus rather than the normative moral claims. Often, the differing approaches come to the same or similar normative moral conclusions, but they do so for very different reasons. For example, one can consider stealing to be morally wrong because the results are bad for society, or because it corrupts the character of the thief, or because it violates a duty each of us has, or because it expresses a lack of responsible care for others, or for other reasons. Although there are variations within each broad category, nonetheless it is helpful to characterize the familiar groupings so that we can see how reason functions within and between them.

It is not unusual for philosophers to consider Socrates if not the first then the greatest early proponent of philosophical ethics. This is because he intensified ancient Greek questioning of tradition, challenging citizens of Athens with rational criticism of practices as well as beliefs, questioning moral as well as scientific claims, and questioning authority, social, political, and even divine. Martyred for his efforts, Socrates remains the paradigm of the philosopher: always looking beneath, behind, and beyond the claims at hand, always challenging authority and questioning assumptions, always expecting reasons to explain and justify beliefs and actions.

With Socrates as the model, Plato, and later his greatest student Aristotle, exemplify the first of the widely recognized approaches to ethics. Of course, there are important differences between their normative ethical views. Nonetheless, what each takes to be central to ethics is the same. The focus is character. For these classical thinkers, living a good life is living a life of integrity, a life committed to excellence, a life demonstrative of courage, wisdom, self-control, justice, friendship, and, to the extent it can be achieved, self-sufficiency, reducing and limiting the effects of chance. The good of a human life rests not so much on the results of our actions or the motives we have for them but on the sort of person we make of ourselves by the way of life we live. Our character is reflected in our *patterns* of behavior, not determined by this or that isolated act or motive. If we want to know what sort of person a given individual is we need to know their characteristic behavior *not* their self-proclaimed moral code. Our values are not merely things we say but are expressed by how we live, remembering, with Aristotle, that one swallow does not make spring, nor does one day make a life.

In his *Republic*, devoted to the question, "What is a good life?" Plato famously distinguishes three aspects of the self, namely, our *appetitive* side, our *spirited* side, and our *rational* side. These correspond to our physical desires for things like food and sex, our emotional needs for things like love and respect, and our intellectual interest in meaning and understanding. For Plato, a good life depends on each aspect of the self doing its part, none trying to do the part of another, and the three being in balance, with reason doing the balancing. Self-control becomes the task of reason, guiding appetite and emotion away from overindulgence. If our rational capacity is too weak, self-control is lost and our lives are consumed with attempting to fill "leaky jars," since, unchecked, both appetite and emotion can never be satisfied. Often Plato is battered for assigning self-control to reason, giving emotion and appetite subservient roles. More often Plato's insistence on all three is lost, as if he thinks that reason is all there is to a human being. For Plato, a good life is becoming a balanced person where understanding guides and harmonizes our physical and emotional inclinations, and reason is expressed in the give-and-take of dialectical conversations captured in the dialogues.

Aristotle's *Nicomachean Ethics* offers a more explicit description of how we are to live. Here, too, a sort of balance is sought through understanding, but for Aristotle the balance is between excess and deficiency. He describes areas of life where moral challenges arise as presenting extremes to avoid by aiming for what he calls the mean. For example, regarding courage, the brave individual avoids both the excessive extreme of taking reckless risks and the defective extreme of avoiding every conceivable risk. Finding and acting on the mean between excessive and defective extremes is the intellectual guide to making yourself a person of excellent character, all, of course, within the context of a community, since humans are social beings.

Plato and Aristotle both reflect the classical Greek notion of *eudaimonia* as the goal for human life. "Happiness" is a common but misleading translation of *eudaimonia*; for ancient Greeks, it means something more like fulfillment, flourishing, living, and doing well, where the activities of a good life are not mere means to contentment but are themselves part of the fulfilling of life.[1] This is why we see Plato and Aristotle frequently dismiss pleasure and glory, things that modern readers often associate with happiness. The goal is to live completely, to experience not merely the pleasures of our animality but the emotional depths and intellectual heights of a fully developed active and aware human being. As Aristotle puts it, "the human good turns out to be the soul's activity that expresses virtue. And if there are more virtues than one, the good will express the best and most complete virtue. Moreover, it will be in a complete life."[2] The Greek word translated here as "virtue" is *arete* and literally means excellence. So, the point is to become an excellent human being, to be virtuous, to live a life constituted by activities expressive of human fulfillment. As a result of this focus on excellence or virtue of human character, this approach to ethical theory has come to be called "virtue ethics."

In *After Virtue*, Alasdair MacIntyre develops a powerful critique of contemporary moral philosophy in which he suggests that our current moral language lacks the contexts from which its significance derives. In the process of developing his critique, he notes that virtue made sense in its original context because ancient Greeks shared beliefs about what it meant to be human and thus about what human excellence was. The context was membership in a community, the Greek city-state, which was the people's guardian and provided a way of life. "Of course all the evidence is that the overwhelming majority of all Greeks, whether Athenian or not, took it for granted that the way of life of their own city was unquestionably the best way of life."[3]

Beyond this strong sense of community, the Greeks had a very broad sense of reason. Clearly, for Plato and Aristotle reason was not conceived narrowly as formal argumentation or empirical verifiability. Using reason meant engaging intellectual capacities, coming up with justifications and explanations for beliefs and practices, drawing on all the resources thinkable, from ordinary experience, literature and the arts, to scholars and common sense. But reason was not just eloquence; reason could help humans discover order in nature. So values were not thought to be relative to each community context but derived their significance from what was taken to be true for any community, based not on a given city-state but on the nature of humans.

The fifteen-hundred-year ecclesiastical dominance of the Western intellectual tradition that followed ancient Greek thought appropriated much of Plato, Aristotle, and their followers, "Christianizing" their ideas into a different take on nature and human nature. Whereas for the Greeks, creation was the interaction of *nous* with *chaos*, mind with disorder, leading to a rationally ordered natural world, Judeo-Christian creation was *ex nihilo*, where God started with nothing and came up with everything by some sort of supernatural magic. The fundamentally different conception of nature and human nature brought with it a fundamentally different approach to ethics. Rather than a focus on human character, on virtue, European medieval ethics centered on human duty revealed by divine commands expressive of natural law, a synthesis of Greek naturalism and Judeo-Christian spirituality.

Deontological ethics, that is, moral systems based on *deontos*, what is binding, necessary, our duty, is a second basic approach to ethics in Western thought. As with other major approaches, deontological ethics takes several forms. The European medieval form is where divine commands reveal human duties. Ethical views based not on divine authority but on assertions of natural rights, increasingly prominent since the seventeenth century and popular among human rights advocates today, are deontological in approach as well. Contemporary proponents would take the United Nations Declaration of Human Rights as stating but not as creating human rights. Rights theories of ethics are duty-based because the role of rights is to recognize binding limits to human interactions based on the content of the rights claims. For example, if every person, by virtue of being human, has a right to participate in the political system governing her or his homeland, then those denied this right have legitimate claims against offenders based in natural moral law, which, like physical law, binds universally. The U.S. founders' appeal to "unalienable rights" was a deontological approach to ethics, asserting that all humans have duties grounded in a necessary respect for natural human rights. The U.S. founders asserted both divine and natural rights claims. Deontological ethics may be ecclesiastical or secular—or both.

The best-known and most influential deontologist in the Western philosophic tradition is Immanuel Kant. Making his early contributions in natural science, Kant's mature philosophical work comes late in his career—and late in the eighteenth century—when he initiates a critical perspective on reason in order to distinguish empty speculation from more valuable philosophic claims. Discouraged by developments in British empiricism culminating in Hume's skepticism on the one hand and by disagreements among Continental rationalists leading to rampant metaphysics on the other, Kant sets out to do a critical study of human reason. Unless we know the limits of human reason, he argued, we will never be able to distinguish knowledge from ignorance. Kant's *Critique of Pure Reason*, his study of what must be true about human beings and what must be true about reality outside of humans in order for science to be possible, stands as one of the most impressive, and difficult, achievements in Western philosophy.

With his *Critique of Practical Reason*, Kant turns to what must be true of human beings and what must be true of external reality for ethics to be meaningful. Elaborated as well in *Foundations of the Metaphysics of Morals*, his system reveals human reason as the grounding for ethics. The function of reason, the purpose for which humans have rational capacity, is, according to Kant, to produce a will good in itself, that is, to make us moral. Kant the natural scientist emerges as the enlightenment thinker par excellence. Duty can be derived directly from reason itself. If humans use their natural capacity for reason, they will not only discover their moral duty but every human will discover the same, universal moral duty, that is, the principle of their actions will at the same time be universalizable without contradiction. Put in what Kant considers a practical formulation, people acting out of respect for duty will treat one another as ends in themselves and never as mere means to other ends. Without getting entangled in the host of controversies surrounding the details of Kant's normative ethics, suffice it to say here that Kant establishes the central, foundational role of abstract rationality in ethics. The influence of this approach is hard to exaggerate. A natural scientific conception of reason is alleged to solve, once and for all, the problem of the ages: how are we to live?

For Kant, "two things fill the mind with ever new and increasing admiration and awe, the oftener and more steadily we reflect on them: the starry heavens above and the moral law within."[4] Scientific reason reveals the laws of nature descriptive of the external world; ethical reason discovers moral truth, subjective because grounded in human reason, yet universal because reason is shared by all humans in virtue of their humanity. Reason modeled after science suggests the possibility of avoiding relativism, be it historical, cultural, or personal. For Kant, ethics based on human reason can achieve universality comparable to the universality of science.

During the same period that varieties of deontological ethics developed in postmedieval Europe, varieties of consequentialist ethics appeared as well. For consequentialism, a third sort of approach to ethical theory, moral decisions are based not on development of character or adherence to duty but on achieving desired ends, on getting certain results, on bringing about particular consequences. Moral duties are of interest only as a means to accomplishing specific goals or end results. With many thinkers contributing along the way, consequentialism reaches its maturity with John Stuart Mill's *Utilitarianism* in the nineteenth century.

Mill works with the central ethical ideas of Jeremy Bentham and others, recognizing the importance of maximizing pleasure and minimizing pain. Elaborating qualitative as well as quantitative differences among pleasures and pains, Mill formulates the principle of utility as a moral directive to bring about the greatest happiness for the greatest number of beings in sentient creation, and to minimize their unhappiness, where happiness is pleasure understood broadly and deeply, and unhappiness is its opposite, namely a wide notion of pain and suffering. To ease the difficulties of making numerous complex calculations regarding the likely consequences of various behavior options, Mill uses the lessons of history to adopt broad rules to guide action, rules that have held up well over time in promoting happiness and minimizing the reverse. Conflicts between rules are resolved by appeal to the principle of utility itself. Utilitarianism has many adherents among contemporary ethical theorists, rivaled in number only by Kantians.

This distinction between duty- and results-based ethics, between deontology and consequentialism, is so pervasive in the Western philosophic tradition for the past several hundred years as to virtually exhaust categories of moral theory. With a passing nod to virtue ethics and divine revelation out of historical curiosity, textbook ethics in the Western tradition have focused overwhelmingly and almost exclusively on these two frameworks.

The opening of the university, increasingly since World War II, to women, people of color, and students from working-class backgrounds has transformed academic ethics. For one thing, it has brought an expanding interest in applied ethics, rarely seen in pre-WWII ethical theory. Articles, books, courses, and even degrees focused on specific areas of application—biomedical ethics, business ethics, ethics and public policy, the ethics of various professions, and so on—are increasingly common. A second aspect of the post-WWII transformation has been the flourishing of various critiques of traditional ethical theory, often from the standpoints of those left out of the tradition. Feminist ethics challenges the traditional universalization of male perspectives noting that women's voices and experiences have been left out. Other critics note the exclusion of people of color from the theoried class and from the traditional cannon, exposing those holding dominant perspectives for presenting themselves as if they speak for all of humanity when their experiences have been exclusive of much of humanity. Critiques anchored in class consciousness, sexual orientation, and ethnicity focus on the differences their inclusion makes to ethical thought, and anthropocentrism is challenged by theorists interested in defending animal rights, a land ethic, environmental protection, and ecological sustainability. While this pluralistic ethical thought is underway, much of it remains marginalized; that is, ethics courses are centered primarily on duty- and results-based views, deontology and consequentialism, with passing references to ancient Greek and medieval ethics, but the perspectives of those left out of the tradition are rarely considered central to the study of ethics. Rather, they tend to be seen as pursuing specific normative ethical agendas.

Perhaps the notable exception is feminist ethics. The sheer numbers of proponents and the impact of quality work over the past generation has led to recognition of the ethics of care as another approach to ethical theory, alongside virtue ethics, deontology, and consequentialism. Carol Gilligan identifies traditional moral reasoning as abstract and hypothetical, concentrating on rights, duties, and consequences, whereas the ethics of care is contextual and narrative, focusing on responsibility. While the tradition tends to view society as a collection of autonomous individuals constrained by rules to control self-interest and aggression, care ethics views society as networks of mutual interdependencies made stable by responsibly addressing people's needs. Gilligan notes that these perspectives have strong gender associations but that they are not gender dependent. Our moral perspectives seem to be more expressions of our experience than functions of human nature.

It is worth noting that the positivist or realist perspective has enjoyed a long development since at least the mid-seventeenth century when Thomas

Hobbes applied scientific reason to the study of human society and found ethics to be derivative of the passions, something humans invent as they rise from the state of nature, a war of each against all wherein there is no right and wrong. According to Hobbes, humans need rules and an enforcer to maximize equal competitors' likelihood of getting what they want, but there is no natural basis for morality; everything is permitted until there are laws forbidding and requiring acts, and humans invent the laws by entering into deals, giving up rights to everything and everyone in exchange for others doing likewise. This grounding of right and wrong in rules that get their authority not from divine or natural moral truth but from human passion and invention is an early form of both the positive law tradition and emotivism. Positive law holds that in the absence of law everything is permitted; law is the grounding for right and wrong. Emotivism is the view that the content of moral claims boils down to emotional approval or disapproval, nothing more. Both function with notions of reason borrowed from empirical science. Neither positive law nor emotivism tend to be considered approaches to ethics per se because they explain ethics away, reducing moral assertions to rules of law or to expressions of sentiment. They contribute to ethical theory in the meta-ethical sense, but take normative ethics to be explained away rather than justified.

If virtue ethics, deontology, consequentialism, and the ethics of care are the predominant frameworks within which ethics is organized in the Western intellectual tradition, what can be said about the role of reason? We have seen the various roles reason plays within each of these approaches: as an intellectual guide to balance and harmony in virtue ethics, as a source of consistent universal moral judgment and logical moral derivations in deontology and as a master of calculation in weighing alternative behavior options for the optimal results in consequentialism. Both the realist or positive law tradition and emotivism conceive reason in its narrow, scientific form and reduce ethics to something else, like rules or expressions of sentiment. In the ethics of care we note a wider sense of reason, one that includes respecting and working with emotion and experience in describing responsible care for those with whom we share our lives.

Reason discovers, derives, calculates, judges, projects implications, balances, and guides. But reason, at least in its scientific form, seems confined to working within rather than between moral frameworks. Deontologists can make sophisticated and powerful arguments demonstrating why the principle from which a particular act is derived cannot be willed as a universal moral law, but their use of reason seems incapable of convincing utilitarians to abandon consequentialism and become deontologists. Likewise, utilitarians can offer rigorous scientific calculations demonstrating the probable outcomes of selected actions, but their reasons for embracing consequentialism are not sufficiently compelling to convert deontologists into consequential-ists. Reason, at least in its calculative and formal argumentative forms, works within but not between moral frameworks. Proponents of the ethics of care acknowledge and underscore the necessity of a broader conception of reason, including emotional and lived experiential influences in efforts to understand ethical reflection and judgment. This is reminiscent of the critiques of tradi-tional ethical thought from Iris Murdoch and Susanne Langer noted in chap-ter one above, that the traditional general approaches to doing ethics exclude important aspects of actual moral reflection.

One has to wonder just how we get ourselves into and out of moral frame-works and whether the traditional approach to describing our ethical thought reflects it accurately. No doubt many of us make most of our moral decisions more-or-less automatically, as extensions of who we are, reflective of our cul-ture, religion, family, personal history, individual convictions, and so on. Some of us may struggle more than others with moral issues, and some of us question standards while others simply accept them. But few of us are purists about these things; we are influenced by a wide variety of sources and most of us would be hard pressed to articulate more than a rough description of our moral perspectives.

A way of describing moral thought independent of the traditional meta-ethical frameworks discussed above is to think in terms of normative ethical perspectives. Often these can function as conceptual structures in terms of which moral issues are interpreted, acting as if they are normative lenses through which issues are seen and engaged. For example, one can think of a traditional moral perspective like "an eye for an eye" as a guide both to le-gitimize and to limit acts of retribution. Another example could be the wide-spread acceptance of slavery in the eighteenth century. Such normative ethi-cal perspectives can function as models or paradigms for individuals and groups. And such paradigms can shift abruptly, as in the case of the familiar and explicit recommendation to change values from an eye for an eye to "turn the other cheek," or the case of a less explicit but radical paradigm shift from embracing slavery as a dominant social institution to finding slavery abhor-rent, as most do today. The world looks different through each of these per-spectives, and genuine adherents behave differently as a result of experienc-ing their lives through these differing moral lenses.

Since specific normative moral perspectives can orient those sharing the perspective to their experience at least as powerfully as any of the traditional metaethical frameworks discussed above, why do philosophers privilege the metaethical account over the normative when organizing ethical thought? That is, why sort ethical views by the grounds offered to explain and defend ethical claims rather than sort them by the normative content of their claims?

Part of the answer may be in the abstract nature of philosophy, always looking beneath, behind, and beyond the claims themselves. Nevertheless, it
would seem that ethical thought could be organized around normative content. For example, ethics could be sorted by the extent to which violence is
accepted, from so-called realism at one extreme (anything goes to get what
you want) to absolute pacifism at the other (violence is never warranted), with
a host of variations justifying degrees of violence between these extremes. In
such an organizational scheme, the reasons in defense of normative claims
would be of interest but would not be the primary organizing principles.

     This issue of whether emphasis belongs on criteria in support of normative
claims or on the normative claims themselves is complex and tricky. It brings
to mind the epistemological problem that Roderick Chisholm called "the
problem of the criterion."[5] Put bluntly, the question for epistemology is
"What is knowledge?" The goal is a criterion. The problem of the criterion
arises because for any candidate we may want to consider, say, for example,
"knowledge is justified true belief," we must test the criterion by checking it
against what we think we know in order to see if the criterion gives us all and
only knowledge claims. We reject the criterion if it lets in claims that should
be excluded (justified true beliefs that are not knowledge) and if it excludes
claims that should be included (knowledge that is not justified true belief).
But—and here is the nub of the problem—how do we know a genuine item
of knowledge to use it as a test case? We cannot reply, "because it is a product of our criterion" since that would make the process circular. But if we
know the genuine cases independently of the criterion, then is the criterion
just a general description of what we think we know and *not* the source and
standard of knowledge that we are looking for? The criterion cannot both generate and rest on the examples.

     Something similar is happening in ethics. How do we arrive at an ethical
claim? Deontologists tell us the claim follows from our duty. Consequential-
ists tell us the claim follows from our best calculations of the likely results.
But why accept either criterion? Presumably because it generates and justifies
claims that we think should be generated and justified. But on what basis do
we think so? The answer cannot return to the examples without presuming
their legitimacy, but that begs the question. It seems that the relationship between any moral criterion and the instances over which it ranges is one of
give and take. We test the criterion against the cases it generates and we test
the cases against the criterion. But, then, we somehow get to moral claims independently of deriving them from a criterion. Above, I suggested that reason
functions within but not between moral frameworks, and when I did so I was
referring to reason in its more scientific, calculative, proof, and evidence
sense. The problem of the criterion seems to suggest that while we can derive

moral claims from various ethical criteria through this sort of reasoning, there must be other ways to get to moral claims in order to have the cases against which we can test our criteria. I think these are identified through the broader forms of reason that Murdoch, Langer, Nussbaum, Gilroy, and others are interested in, and it is this more comprehensive sense of moral thought that I want to explore.

Introductory ethics textbooks always include Kant and Mill, deontology, and consequentialism, sometimes they include proponents of feminist ethics, but they rarely include the work of or reference to Mohandas Gandhi and Martin Luther King, Jr., two moral giants of the twentieth century. Why? Is it because Gandhi and King were activists in social movements, because they challenged dominant systems on behalf of aggrieved people with little power, because they operated outside of traditional academic structures, or because they were proponents of nonviolence, a normative ethical view that is rarely reflected in traditional ethics? Perhaps it is for all of these reasons or for none of them. But it seems odd for academic ethics largely to ignore figures of such moral enormity, whether we share their convictions or not. Perhaps they are not embraced by traditional ethical theory because their views challenge the dominant discourse within the tradition or because that discourse is so entrenched that it determines the questions and issues that can be addressed and subsequently leaves nonviolence out. Whatever the reasons, this is a case of the problem of the criterion; if ethical theory is to account for moral thought, it must accommodate the work of important contributors to morality. We need to widen our look at what counts as legitimate sources, examples, and ingredients in ethical thought.

In *Philosophy in a New Key*, Susanne Langer addresses a similar concern. Working in an era dominated by philosophical enthusiasm for scientific reasoning, Langer respects the achievements of science and of modeling scientific thought in philosophy, but she is convinced that "not only science, but myth, analogy, metaphorical thinking, and art are intellectual activities"[6] as well, and that philosophy should not be stuck in the shadow of empirical science. She seeks a reconsideration of human needs beyond the inventory of natural science, beyond physical demands in service to survival. For Langer, humans typically need meaning and need to express ideas through values, ritual, art, laughter, speech, and weeping, in addition to science. Unwilling to accept Wittgenstein's admonition to pass over in silence that of which we cannot speak, and rejecting Carnap's emotivist accounts of cries and lyrical verse, Langer tells us that meaning is wider than language but that access is blocked by two dogmas of scientific epistemology: "(1) That language is the only means of articulating thought, and (2) That everything which is not speakable thought is feeling. . . . [S]o long as we admit only discursive symbolism as a bearer of ideas, 'thought' in this restricted sense must be regarded as our only intellectual activity."[7] Langer doubts that thought is limited to discursive language and she explicitly rejects the notion that whatever cannot be expressed linguistically is necessarily inconceivable, ineffable, emotional, or mystical. Some ideas require nondiscursive forms of conception and expression.

For Langer, "the conditions for rationality lie deep in our pure animal experience—in our power of perceiving, in the elementary functions of our eyes and ears and fingers." "[S]ince no experience occurs more than once," she argues, "so-called 'repeated' experiences are really *analogous* occurrences, all fitting a form that was abstracted on the first occasion."[8] This is why we see things rather than sense data; we abstract a form from each experience and use it to conceive the experience as a whole. Experience, in this view, is not a passive process of gathering and storing data; experiencing is itself a process of formulation. Langer invites us "to tackle anew, and with entirely different expectations, the whole problem of the limits of reason," bringing within the realm of reason much that has traditionally been excluded. In her view, aesthetic attraction and mysterious fear are probably the first manifestations of the mental function that leads to the power of conception and the development of speech.[9] The capacity to recognize analogous experience, the beginning of abstraction, is akin to metaphor, the abstractive seeing of new relationships that runs ahead of language. Metaphors catch on, become familiar, fade from figurative to literal use, and become part of discursive language. Her point is that humans have experiences, ideas, and conceptions ahead of the development of language adequate to express them. This is why taking science, scientific language, and scientific reasoning as the model for moral thought is mistaken. It is not only too narrow an understanding of reason; it is backward. That is, ethics is not merely sloppy science; ethics is working at human phenomena for which precise, explicit, discursive language is not yet fully available. Rather than expecting ethics to be reducible to the terms of scientific reasoning, terms at the advanced stage of explicit discourse, we need to explore the phenomena of ethics on their own terms, using forms of expression adequate to those phenomena, regardless of whether the expressions are adequate to strictures on language purported to be required in modern science.

It makes no sense to condemn ethics for not being science, nor does it make sense to caricature reason in narrow, modern, scientific terms and relegate all other thought to irrationality. Recognizing a wider set of forms of reason, wherein science involves one subset among many, opens the study of values to sources rarely consulted by most traditional ethical theorists and makes possible a wider understanding of the give and take between traditional moral criteria and the cases against which they must be tested. Given the direction the tradition has taken for the last few hundred years, and given the problems the tradition faces in meeting its own expectations for reasons and evidence — problems like those identified by Rorty and McIntyre noted above — an exploration of ethical sources within this wider conception of reason is in order. The first such source to be considered below is where we encounter both the "aesthetic attraction" and the "mysterious fear" mentioned above, namely, in lived experience.

NOTES

1. Nussbaum, Martha, *The Fragility of Goodness* (New York: Cambridge University Press, 1986), 6n.

2. Aristotle, *Nicomachean Ethics* (1098a), 16–19.

3. MacIntyre, Aladsair, *After Virtue* (Notre Dame, IN: University of Notre Dame Press, 1981), 133.

4. Kant, Immanuel, *The Critique of Practical Reason*, tr. Lewis White Beck (Indianapolis: Bobbs-Merrill, 1956, originally published in 1788), 166.

5. Chisholm, Roderick M., *Theory of Knowledge* (Englewood Cliffs, NJ: Prentice Hall, 1966), 56ff.

6. Langer, Susanne K., *Philosophy in a New Key* (Cambridge, MA: Harvard University Press, 1942; 3rd edition, 1957), xiii.

7. Langer, *Philosophy in a New Key*, 87–88.

8. Langer, *Philosophy in a New Key*, 89.

9. Langer, *Philosophy in a New Key*, 97, 110.

Chapter Three

Experience in Context

Text without context is pretext.

—Marion Wright Edelman

If we have learned anything from the various contemporary critiques of the Western intellectual tradition, it is that it must include the recognition that every assertion, every claim, every statement comes from a perspective; there is no neutral point from which to think and speak. Ideas happen in history, in specific times and places, in relationship with events and other ideas surrounding them. We understand "ethics" to derive from *ethos*, way of life, and we have seen Aristotle acknowledge the importance of the way of life each of us has known as we have grown up; we cannot escape the influence our history has on our values. The problem, then, is how to talk about lived experience and its influence on ethics without begging the question, without our biases influencing—even becoming—the outcome. Since there is no neutral point from which to begin, the best we can do is admit our biases, maintain a persistent self-criticism about our perspectives, entertain a broad range of options as open-mindedly as possible, and minimize the extent to which however we begin limits our work. Awareness of the problem is a large part of addressing it.

Rather than begin with ancient Greeks, medieval religious views, Enlightenment rationality, or a modern or postmodern take on values, I want to go back to about 11,000 BCE, to the time when humans, around the globe, were all hunter-gatherers. In *Guns, Germs and Steel: The Fates of Human Societies*, Jared Diamond asks why history unfolded differently on different continents. Noting that most attempts to answer the question have focused on literate Western Eurasian and North American societies, Diamond points out

29

that humans have only been writing since 3,000 BCE. So the question becomes, why did Western Eurasian and North American societies arise and
dominate? Capitalism, science, technology, and so on, are proximate answers
only (i.e., why do they arise in Western European and North American societies rather than in Australia, Central America, or sub-Saharan Africa?). Why
did wealth and power come to be distributed as they are now rather than in
some other way? Why did human development proceed at such different rates
on different continents?[1]

Diamond is a physiologist who both embraces natural selection as an explanatory tool and is highly suspicious of the traditional racist explanations
for the triumph of Europeans over, say, Aboriginal Australians. Yes, Aborigi-
nals hunted and gathered for 40,000 years and Europeans dominated them in
just a generation, with steel tools and centralized political structure. But
"stone age" people are as intelligent as "advanced" people. The answer to the
big question about continental variation of human development is not found
in skin color or hair texture. As we now know, those who developed to take
dominant positions had the guns, steel tools, and immunity to diseases that
decimated indigenous hunter-gatherers—immunity that is accounted for by
association with domesticated animals. Why did development not happen the
other way around, with sub-Saharan Africans, Aztecs, Mayans, or Maori end-
ing up dominant and Europeans subordinate?

Diamond's thesis is that history followed different courses for different
peoples because of environmental differences, not because of genetic superiority of some people over others. He considers human development from origins in Africa 7 million years BCE to the present, emphasizing the last dozen
millennia. For Diamond, the key to understanding development variation by
continent is in understanding food production. Development of science, technology, written language, centralized economies, centralized political systems, and more all follow a people's transition from hunter-gatherers to food
producers. Due to geographic and geological variations and uneven distribution of domesticable plant and animal species, independent domestication of
plants and animals arises at widely different times, hundreds of years sooner
in the fertile crescent of the Middle East than in the Western hemisphere, and
is dispersed at widely different rates, primarily due to the East-West axis of
distribution in Eurasia compared with the North-South axis of Central America. Consequently, Europeans took some of their developmental advantages
with them when they ventured forth, and the advantages made all the difference.

Certainly indigenous North Americans quickly developed great skills with
horses and guns once they had access to them; their disadvantages had to
do not with differences between European and North American peoples but

with differences in access to a particular domesticated animal species and to firearms technology. Something very similar can be said for every other subordinated group of people. Intercultural "superiority" (i.e., a "winning" record in cross-cultural collisions) reflects access to advantages like guns, immunity to epidemic diseases, and so on, and does not reflect biological superiority of one people over another or "manifest destiny."

An interesting aspect of Diamond's outlook is his claim that huntergatherers, bands, and tribes (i.e., relatively small, independent groups) tend toward egalitarianism as a political value, while chiefdoms, kingdoms, and states (i.e., relatively large interrelated groups) tend to hierarchy and bureaucracy as they develop centralized political systems. Smaller groups evolve into larger ones either by conquest or by joining into collectives for defense against a common enemy. Diamond sees religion and ideology arising and evolving to hold these ever larger groups together, typically, he says, to support what he takes to be the end of the evolutionary process (so far) regarding politics: kleptocracy, rule by the systematic theft of everything of value from the many and concentrating wealth and power in the hands of a few. One can only wonder what ethics might mean in this context—not the sort of question Diamond addresses.

What has all of this to do with ethics and experience? We need to recognize context as important to any understanding of experience. While admittedly atypical for discussions of ethics, a broad view of human development over the past 13,000 years offers a context even for the more usually considered contexts: the cultural variations in the contemporary mix. At the same time, this approach leaves us wondering whether human history is nothing more than the inevitable process of natural selection, where humanity may as well be a set of bee hives or ant colonies, where geographic determinism simply plays itself out and we puzzle over whether human questions of meaning and value themselves have meaning and value. In nearly five hundred pages, Diamond never mentions ethics or meaning, and he downplays human culture as more a by-product of an inevitable process than anything with explanatory significance. While I am inclined to part ways with Diamond on both issues, I find his wide contextualization helpful not only for disabusing us of presumptions of superiority and inferiority, but also because it challenges us to resist privileging any cultural perspective over any other. The variables are so many, the issues so complex, the stakes so high, and the intellectual tools themselves so questionable that we can feel overwhelmed. The temptation is to give up, to settle for our own private dogma as so many people seem to do, all too often imposing it on everyone else. The other common alternative is to insist that every answer is as good as every other and embrace a thoroughgoing relativism; this has become the more fashionable choice in educated circles. Yet it is just this sort of broad ground-clearing we have seen from Diamond that provides a third option, a way to avoid both dogmatism and relativism, an opening for a fresh look at how lived experience contributes to our moral perspectives.

Keeping in mind Langer's suggestion that thought and meaning can run out ahead of our linguistic capacity for expression and her insight that humans value more than survival and the necessities that sustain it, we need to consider how bits of lived experience give rise to moral reflections. We need to identify experiences of "aesthetic attraction" and "mysterious fear" that may bear relevance to embracing a moral vision.

"Value" has its etymological root in *valere*, to be of worth. Our values express whatever we find to be of worth. In his seventeenth-century scientific study of human values in *Leviathan*, Thomas Hobbes identifies a "state of nature" not unlike the account Diamond offers in *Guns, Germs and Steel*. For Hobbes, the natural condition of humanity is the war of each against all, where human life is "nasty, brutish and short" until humans invent rules and empower an enforcer to maximize their likelihood of getting and keeping what they want. But the problem with this foundation for values—in Hobbes, Diamond, and others—is that it assumes that survival and conditions supporting it are all that matter to human beings. As we have seen above, a variety of critics of ethics modeled after scientific reason have suggested that moral thinking reflects human interests, values, and concerns beyond biological necessity and beyond calculative and proof-oriented aspects of reason. As Nussbaum noted in her discussion of Aristotle, asking "How are we to live?" in Aristotle's world was a question in search of human fulfillment, flourishing, not simply life, but a good life. Murdoch, Langer, and Gilroy all reject the narrow conception of reason and its restrictions as well, and they do so in order to offer accounts of human values more accurate to their experiences and reflections on human fulfillment.

Langer cites myth, ritual, art, metaphorical thought, speech, music, laughter, and weeping, in addition to science, as meaningful expressions, conceding that among them, only science can meet the positivist criterion of meaning. The others are not clearly empirically verifiable or meaningful in virtue of the terms used to express them. Rather than accept only science as meaningful, Langer suspects that the criterion is inadequate, an instance of what later comes to be called the problem of the criterion. It is not that the criterion is wrong but that it is too narrow; the limits of the criterion need not inhibit a serious look at meaning beyond science.

In *The Power of Myth*, Joseph Campbell takes a similarly broad and open look at the big question humans have struggled over, "How are we to live?" For Campbell, humans as far back as we have evidence seem to have interpreted their experiences and expressed them in stories that give form to life. Myths, across cultures, tend to deal with the maturation of the individual, from dependency through adulthood, through maturity to death, relating individuals to the group and relating the group to nature and the cosmos. Myths express wonder and awe at life itself, offer a vision of the natural order of things, validate the social order from which they come, and teach how life should be lived. Such stories arise out of realizations that members of the group have had, realizations that need expression whether or not available means of articulation are adequate.[2] They are products not of individuals but of communities, expressing shared values and shared vision. Yet they reflect the cumulative experience of the group, direct and indirect, as it is passed through generations. Myths are stories about the wisdom of life within the contexts from which they come. They are not literal but metaphorical and thus are lost if taken literally; they are expressions of likenesses that are important but not always seen, patterns that situate individuals within their cultural contexts, that help group members accept the realities in which they live, negotiate the difficulties they face, and flourish to the extent they can. And, Campbell tells us, those who told the stories did not take them to be literally true, perhaps because they knew the literal truth was beyond them. Myths are not mere superstitions, "magic" solutions to unanswerable questions; if they were, they would just be bad science. Myths are not science at all, and not attempts at science. The purpose of a myth is not knowledge but wisdom, not a literal explanation of facts but a guide to good judgment. For Campbell, categorizing given stories as myths has no negative connotations. In his view, stories from the various religious traditions of the world are myths, their importance demonstrated by the ways of life of their practitioners. "Religion," after all, is derived from *religio*, that which binds together.

Too often myths are dismissed as untrue, as if they were made to describe facts or actual events rather than teach group wisdom. Perhaps this is because myths, like any other cultural product, are time and place bound, often expressing one set of values toward the in-group and quite another for outsiders. This is a main reason for cultural, religious, and ethnic collisions; values that developed and were embraced in specific times and places bump into one another as populations grow and as communications and transportation expand. Group wisdom for a given context may not effectively transfer to another, and it may not be welcome. The social inertia of traditions tends to reinforce defensiveness against outsider wisdom. The contemporary cosmopolitan view of the variety of myths, and with them of cultures and values, awareness largely inspired by exposure to the social sciences, may be a large part of the widespread embrace of value relativism. On the other hand, people with limited access to the big picture of multiple cultures, religions, and values are less likely to entertain relativism. Compared with the seeming self-centeredness of dogmatism, relativism looks downright sophisticated. Yet, one cannot help but wonder whether the choice is limited to these two options.

For Campbell, "myth is a manifestation in symbolic images, in metaphorical images, of the energies of the organs of the body in conflict with each other. This organ wants this, that organ wants that. The brain is one of the organs."[3] He goes on to say that the imagination is grounded in the organs of the body, and since these are the same in all human beings, there is a common denominator for a myth based not on religion, nationality, region, or language but on our common ground: humans come from the earth and were not put here from elsewhere but are of the earth, are the consciousness of the earth. But the society such a myth would have to talk about "is the society of the planet. And until that gets going, you don't have anything."[4] Until global conversations reflect and respect all perspectives, and until realizations regarding the flourishing *of the whole* are widely expressed and valued as wisdom, there is no context for a universal myth. Two things can be drawn from this: first, the realization that cross-cultural wisdom is at least possible, a meaningful ideal toward which to aspire, and second, that the "truth" of a myth is a matter of how well it serves members of its community with the needed wisdom to accept contextual realities, negotiate difficulties, and live good lives.

Myths are not ethics, but their relevance to ethics should be obvious, since they express the collective wisdom of cultures on how life should be lived. In this sense myths are proto-ethics, metaphoric expressions of what ethics attempts to make discursive and explicit. No wonder Nussbaum was nonplussed that ancient Greek drama and poetry were segregated from ancient Greek philosophy in the scholarship of her graduate school days; the very material on which the ethical thought rested, the cultural wisdom in which the philosophers themselves were nurtured, was at the heart of the ethical theories developed. No one reading Plato could miss the constant references to myth, drama, poetry, music, epic, and the way of life for ordinary Athenians. And Aristotle explicitly insists on both respecting the context of our upbringing and expecting levels of precision in reasoning appropriate to the subject, with math and science employing different forms of reason than ethics and the arts. Yet our own ethical theorists, at least since the Enlightenment, have for the most part followed the patterns of specialization prompted by the remarkable achievements of natural science and technology and have become increasingly detached from the broader cultural influences on our ways of life, and especially on how they relate to the question "How are we to live?" The subsequent work in ethical theory is often highly abstract, esoteric, and very tightly argued, with a fairly small number of participants in increasingly jargonized and erudite professional conversations.

Meanwhile, moral events outpace academic ethics. Slavery is gradually abolished and becomes abhorrent globally (in principle if not completely in practice), and women's suffrage becomes a worldwide standard of democracy, yet issues of race and gender are not typical features of academic ethics until generations later, to this day often requiring advocates for their curricular inclusion. Gandhi and King make their contributions to the collective moral life, violence is nearly universally condemned (sadly, acts of violence are so "wrong" that they are taken to warrant violent retaliatory responses, according to conventional values), and yet these moral giants do not find their way into mainstream ethical theory. Nonviolence is not typically mentioned in ethics textbooks. Perhaps things are beginning to change, with the feminist critique first challenging and increasingly moving into mainstream academic philosophy, encouraging a wide range of critiques from people at the margins, from diverse racial, class-consciousness, sexual orientation, environmental, and other perspectives, and bringing along more inclusive forms of reason as well as an interest in applied ethics.

Of course, every experience happens within a context, so the dominant vision of the context has a role in the interpretation of each experience. Sometimes events are filtered through dominant cultural values, making them acceptable to those having the experiences; but sometimes the events are in such dissonance with dominant cultural values in the minds of those experiencing them that they provoke reactions against conventional wisdom. Whether or not the discursive language is adequate to the experience, experiences that lead to realizations demanding expression always generate stories, photographs, poems, gestures, paintings, songs, cries, films, and more, many of which animate the imaginations of others sufficiently to impact ethics. So we must look at both the direct experiences themselves to ask why they prompt us to reflect on their ethical import and we must look at what might be called indirect experiences, the experiences not of the immediate occasions but of their expressions in their various forms. Both contribute to ethics.

Langer has told us that experiences with meaning import that we do not have adequate conventional language to express lead us to metaphoric expression, to suggesting a likeness that has gone unnoticed. Setting aside the notion of metaphor for now, we need to ask first what are these experiences that have meaning import? For the diverse range of critics I cited above, the question "How are we to live?" involves more than survival. The hope is for lives that flourish, lives that thrive individually and collectively. The hope is for a good life, in the broadest and deepest sense that such a notion can have. Presumably it was realizations based in experiences with meaning import that led to the generation of myths in ancient societies and that encourage mythmaking—storytelling—still. What are examples of such experiences? I suspect they are shared by all of us in our ordinary lives, experiences of what Langer calls "aesthetic attraction," a perceptual satisfaction or liking, such as loving relationships manifest in everyday events, and also experiences of "mysterious fear," of a threatening natural force, for instance. The implications for ethics, for "the right course of life" are clear, namely, to cherish and protect loving relationships and to be wary of perceived threats. Whatever we find to be of worth reflects our values, remembering that how we act is a more accurate account than what we say.

Perhaps the direct experiences having the most immediate impact on our values are those with which we grow up, those providing feelings of safety and security as well as those presenting trauma. Direct experiences can affect us profoundly because they engage us wholly, including physical, emotional, social, and personal aspects, as well as intellectual. Parents, siblings, extended family members, neighbors, and friends—all who are part of our lives in our youth—contribute in large and small ways to our perceptions of well-being or its absence, and, consequently, to our value formation. It is a truism that role models are significant contributors to the value perspectives we take, yet references to the significance of moral role models, while notable in Plato and Aristotle, are nearly absent in modern ethical theory. Academics sometimes acknowledge, in prefaces or footnotes, indebtedness to influential professors with whom they studied, yet such references in ethical theory itself are unheard of.

In a similar vein, traumatic experiences have a life-altering impact on many individuals, yet rarely are these central in ethical theory. For example, Elie Wiesel's moving stories of life in Nazi death camps, based on his own life experience, are respectfully categorized out of the philosophy curriculum into literature. My point is not that such stories are ethical theory; they are not. Rather, my point is that the *experiences* that led to such literary expressions are themselves the material of ethics, yet such experiences tend to be set aside as anecdotal by ethical theorists. Again we see reason modeled after science. Of course, there are academic philosophers who teach courses in philosophy and literature in which they use literary texts as material for philosophic insight, and there are academics who use literary or historic texts as materials of study in ethics, to provide cases of moral struggle. Nonetheless, ethical theorists avoid introducing reflections on their own personal experience as they do their work, even though such experiences may have contributed greatly to their own moral perspectives.

All of us experience what we might call "moral horror" at various points in our lives, direct encounters with people or events so morally disgusting or repulsive that they both defy discursive description and impress their import on our values. Perhaps this is why, when retelling a personal experience of moral horror, we often say, "you had to be there to understand." Instances of physical, sexual, or psychological abuse; cases of extreme cruelty; suffering of innocents; episodes of racism, sexism, heterosexism, torture, or neglect; and experiences of poverty, hunger, exploitation, untreated disease, and more can all provoke visceral reactions and leave lasting impressions on who we are. Sometimes mass media allow millions to witness moral horror, like the televised beating of Rodney King by police officers in 1991, or the live broadcast of the collapse of the World Trade Towers in New York City after the murder-suicide attacks of September 11, 2001. The sense of moral revulsion can be so strong that many witnesses report feeling as though the events were not happening at all, that they were somehow simulated for television, that they could not be real. Moral horror not only leaves an indelible mark, but often prompts a felt need to "do something" in response to the horror. This is especially relevant to our moral lives since episodes of moral horror often become the conditions we cite to relax our own moral restraints in order to respond, often, to retaliate. So, the influence of moral horror on our moral perspectives both contributes to our sense of wrong and can be used to justify a righteous response. Clearly, experiences of moral horror impact our moral vision.

What would it look like for ethical theorists to acknowledge and reflect on lived experiential influences that impacted their own moral positions? There are notable examples, though they are exceptions to mainstream philosophy and usually come into the discipline from the outside, voices from those who had been excluded from the ranks of philosophers. W. E. B. DuBois comes to mind immediately. A student of William James at Harvard in the late nineteenth century, DuBois has only in the last couple of decades begun to be cited as an important contributor to philosophy and to moral thought. His work is rarely part of textbook ethics. *The Souls of Black Folk* opens with a powerful discussion of conceptual issues crucial to understanding race in America and is clearly grounded in DuBois's personal experiences living in this country as a black man. His moral vision was profoundly affected by his day-to-day encounters with the real question, "How does it feel to be a problem?" He tells of being shut out from the dominant culture by a veil, yet being gifted with a necessary second sight, seeing not only others but seeing how he is seen. He describes the peculiar sensation of double-consciousness, "always looking at one's self through the eyes of others, measuring one's soul by the tape of a world that looks on in contempt and pity." He expresses his longing "to merge his double self into a better and truer self," wishing "neither of the older selves to be lost."[5] It is hard to imagine philosophical considerations of race not grounded in lived experience; perhaps neglect of experiential contributions to moral thought has reinforced neglect of race in mainstream philosophical considerations.

Feminist Theory: From Margin to Center, bell hooks's powerful book ex-
amining central issues in sexual politics, comes to mind as well. Hooks's
lived experience drives and animates her theorizing about gender, race, economics, parenting, politics, and violence. She frequently breaks the philosopher's rule against using the first-person pronoun, for example:

> My awareness of feminist struggle was stimulated by social circumstance.
> Growing up in a Southern, black, father-dominated, working-class household, I
> experienced . . . varying degrees of patriarchal tyranny and it made me angry—
> it made us all angry. Anger led me to question the politics of male dominance
> and enabled me to resist sexist socialization.[6]

Readers of hooks cannot miss her eagerness to think through social, political,
and ethical issues unrestrained by traditional narrow conceptions of reason.
Of course anger is relevant; of course day-to-day lived experience of very ordinary people is relevant; of course mundane workplace issues are relevant;
of course aesthetic dimensions of experience are relevant. These are both the
sources from which moral thoughts arise and the test cases against which the
adequacy of moral thinking is judged.

As I reflect on examples of ethical theorists who use personal lived experience centrally in their work, I am struck by two things: they tend to be working at the outer edges rather than the mainstream of philosophy and their contributions have either been made in the recent generation, or, if made earlier,
the work has been brought into philosophic legitimacy in the recent generation. And very often such contributions have come from outsider wisdom,
from women, people of color, sometimes from outside Europe and North
America, and so on. I have in mind things like Sara Ruddick's *Maternal
Thinking: Toward a Politics of Peace*, where practices of mothering inform
social ethics; Marilyn Frye's *The Politics of Reality: Essays in Feminist Theory*, in which frustration and anger are probed for insights about injustice;
Franz Fanon's *The Wretched of the Earth*, wherein a voice of the colonized
reveals a perspective forged in exploitation; and much more. I suspect the ir-
relevance of mainstream ethical theory to personal experience is greater for
those at the edges of or outside mainstream thought, largely because dominant views are both presented as and taken to be "normal." If Langer is on to
something, experiences of import, especially those outside the mainstream
"norms," demand expression even if conventional means of expression are
inadequate, and even if mainstream ethical theory is not particularly encouraging or receptive. So, new and creative expressions of insights that both
challenge and contribute to mainstream thought are born, in part because outsiders see things that insiders cannot see. As DuBois suggested, they have to
in order to survive as outsiders.

Thinking about philosophical insight arising out of lived experience brings to mind a comment Marilyn Frye makes at the start of her now well-known essay, "Sexism," from *The Politics of Reality*, where she says, "teaching philosophy had already taught me that people cannot be persuaded of things they are not ready to be persuaded of; there are certain perplexities of will and prior experience which will inevitably block persuasion, no matter the merits of the case presented."[7] In raising the relationship between lived experience ("perplexities of will and prior experience") and philosophy ("the merits of the case presented"), Frye alerts us to a distinction academic philosophers well know but rarely discuss, namely, that between simply living our lives on the one hand, and doing philosophy on the other. I have already noted what I take to be the drift in the history of Western philosophy since the Enlightenment, to increasingly narrow notions of reason modeled after science, widening the distance between lived experience and theory. Mainstream contemporary philosophy tends to be removed from, tends to distance itself from, ordinary lived experience. I am inclined to see this issue with one of my former teachers, Roderick Chisholm, who says, in his Carus Lectures, "whatever we are justified in assuming when we are not doing philosophy, we are also justified in assuming when we *are* doing philosophy."[8]

When I begin to think about ways that my own lived experience has influenced my philosophical reflections, examples come easily. Spending four years on crutches from age thirteen to seventeen, including a year in a school for the "handicapped," taught me the meaning of segregation beyond a dictionary definition. I never grasped the concept of class difference until I took my blue-collar-raised self from a little-known Midwestern liberal arts college to New England for a Ph.D. program in an Ivy League institution. One could hardly avoid confronting class issues at every turn at Brown University in the late 1960s and early 1970s, and often race was in tow as well. Similarly, I was at a loss to conceptualize nonviolence prior to encounters with both the civil rights and antiwar movements in my community, on campus, and via television, during college and graduate school. Readers who are old enough will recall that such issues were deemed inappropriate for classroom education at the time they were happening; my civil rights and antiwar lives had to be separate from my academic life. Gender inequities and sexual orientation discrimination were driven home experientially as well. One could get into them just so far in the abstract, but experiencing injustices in the lives of family and friends is a basis for convictions. In an effort to deepen my grasp of ethical issues related to so-called developing nations and to strengthen my efforts to teach ethical issues related to international development, I left the overdeveloped world to visit the "third world," and, convinced of the importance of direct experience, revised my course to include a two-week immersion for my students, hosted by and working with local folks on a community project in rural interior Jamaica. Even such a contrived experience can generate more learning than would endless hours in a library studying development literature. Presumably these are the sorts of experiences Frye has in mind when she talks about "being ready to be persuaded." The experiences alone do not entail particular values, but the experiences challenge our conceptual frameworks, widen our perspectives, and open us to reflection. A diverse set of experiences can ready us to question what we take as given and may even provoke fundamental ethical shifts between metaethical frameworks.

One has to wonder why academic philosophy has paid such experiences so little heed. Somehow ethical theory drifted more and more toward abstract, detached, argumentative, and hypothetical considerations of moral issues, widening the distance from lived experience. Yet it seems that reason in this restricted sense settles few ethical disputes, working better *within* ethical frameworks than *between* them. It can provide derivations from Kant's categorical imperative or from Mill's version of utility but it does not help us choose between Kant and Mill. Yet it seems that lived experience sometimes provokes fundamental ethical shifts. I am not saying that *only* lived experience does so or that it *always* does so; but it seems too significant to neglect if we are to understand moral reasoning broadly and accurately. Using "reason" nontechnically, it is reasonable to expect more-or-less rational people to draw logical conclusions from their lived experience; in fact, we would regard folks as deficient in rationality were they not to do so. Yet, somehow academic philosophy has managed to get so caught up in the analysis of concepts and the formulation of arguments and evidence that we often detach ourselves from the practices, traditions, habits, and patterns of behavior that shape the perspectives within which we think and work. And while the more technical, narrower notion of reason has been of greater interest to academic philosophers, the broader, more ordinary notion of reason remains deeply influential over fundamental convictions, a notion not only wide enough for experiences of ethical import, but including aesthetic, metaphoric, artistic, and other forms of thought as well.

I began this chapter by contextualizing this discussion within a wide sweep of many thousands of years of human development. I would like to conclude it by considering the more immediate geopolitical context of our ethical thought, global development for the past fifty years.

Development discourse, the practice of talking about the world by reference to "developed" and "underdeveloped" countries, came into use with President Harry Truman's inaugural address, January 20, 1949: "We must embark on a bold new program for making the benefits of our scientific advances and industrial progress available for the improvement and growth of underdeveloped areas." Assuring listeners that he was not suggesting "the old imperialism—exploitation for foreign profit," Truman looked toward a "program of development based on the concepts of democratic fair-dealing."[9] As many critics of development see it, billions of people became underdeveloped by Truman's declaration. "In a real sense, from that time on, they ceased being what they were, in all their diversity, and were transmogrified into an inverted mirror of others' reality: a mirror that belittles them and sends them off to the end of the queue. . . . Since then, development has connoted at least one thing: to escape from the undignified condition called underdevelopment."[10]

Given the realities of the intensifying Cold War at the close of World War II, the practical upshot of Truman's vision was a contest between the Western European and North American allies on the one hand, and the Soviet Union on the other. The superpowers offered development assistance to the rest of the world and had their own spheres of influence in mind; in Jared Diamond's terms, the geophysically advantaged used their advantages to gain further advantage. The "first world," Western capitalist nations, struggled with the "second world," the Soviet bloc, over the "third world," everyone else. Political, military, and economic power were at stake. The political liberation movement following WWII, in which colonies pursued independence from colonial powers, led to new political alignments and often to neocolonialism. Development became a euphemism for wealthier nations and multinational corporations entering third-world countries in search of natural resources, new markets for their products, and cheap labor to reduce production costs. Development came to mean economic growth, ultimately growth in income per person, losing any remnant of the ancient Greek notion of *eudaimonia*, human fulfillment. Economic value overwhelmed and subsumed all other values as regional and subsistence economies, which had sustained populations for centuries, were replaced by a global market economy. The commons have become resources, men and women—and children—have become labor, and traditional wisdom has become an obstacle to economic "progress." With development as it has been practiced, "the unity of the world is realized through its Westernization. By the mid-twentieth century, the term 'underdeveloped' had taken the place of 'savages.' Economic performance had replaced reason as the measure of [hu]man[s] . . . [and] world society has to be achieved through improvement of the backward."[11] Sadly, Truman's vision was mistaken. Fifty years of development has, in fact, continued the transfer of wealth from poorer third-world to wealthier first-world nations, just as had been the practice during colonialism.[12]

Ironically, to model global development after the economic progress of Western Europe and North America is to project disaster, since, "if all countries 'successfully' followed the industrial example, five or six planets would be needed to serve as mines and waste dumps."[13] Needless to say, five or six planets like ours are not available. Not only is the Western model not sustainable, but the more "successful" the West is in bringing more and more nations "up" to our levels of consumption, the greater the demands on nonrenewable resources, thus driving prices ever higher for everyone and hastening the point of resource depletion, for the first and second worlds as well as the third.

Where is ethical theory in all of this? Where indeed. When traditional values are crowded out of influence by either a frenzy for economic gain or a desperation for the means of subsistence, moral concerns fade in practice, leaving less for ethical theory to theorize about. Cornel West has called attention to just this drift in contemporary society, the undermining of traditional morality by corporate market institutions, with profit as the preeminent value, seducing the public to a culture of consumption, using comfort, convenience, and sexual stimulation to reduce individuals to objects of pleasure. This is "especially evident in the culture industries—television, radio, video, music—in which gestures of sexual foreplay and orgiastic pleasure flood the market place . . . and thereby edge out nonmarket values—love, care, service to others—handed down by preceding generations."[14] Without nonmarket values like self-love, love of others, kindness, and care, West sees no basis for hope. Although West's focus is our own moral collapse, something analogous is happening globally.

According to Wolfgang Sachs, there were roughly 5,100 languages spoken around the globe in 1992. "Just under 99 percent of them are native to Asia, Africa, the Pacific and the American continents, while a mere 1 percent find their homes in Europe."[15] Expectations are that "within a generation or two not many more than 100 of these languages will survive." Of course, with the demise of languages, entire cultures vanish. As Sachs puts it, "the homogination of the world is in full swing. A global monoculture spreads like an oil slick over the entire planet."[16] How could more than five thousand languages survive to the brink of the third millennium yet just 2 percent be expected to survive another half-century? Sachs argues that by the end of the eighteenth century, traditional notions of peace as the fruit of justice had given way to the Enlightenment suggestion that peace would result from mankind united under the achievements of civilization. In the Preamble to the United Nations Declaration, the quest for peace was linked to the hope for advancement of peoples around the globe, "a royal road to progress on which all peoples converge."[17] Again, the values of the market overwhelm all other values. Ivan Illich goes so far as to claim that "commitment to progress has extinguished the possibility of an agreed setting within which a search for the common good can arise."[18]

All values being reduced to those of the market finds articulate resistance from Gandhi:

I do not believe that multiplication of wants and of machinery contrived to supply them is taking the world a single step nearer its goal. . . . I wholeheartedly detest this mad desire to destroy distance and time, to increase animal appetites and go to the ends of the earth in search of their satisfaction. If modern civilization stands for all this, and I have understood it to do so, I call it Satanic.

He goes on, "it is theft for me to take any fruit that I do not need, or to take it in larger quantity than is necessary. We are not always aware of our real needs, and most of us improperly multiply our wants and thus unconsciously make thieves of ourselves."[19] In this analysis, one implication of the current global development context within which moral thought happens is that development, as it is practiced and experienced by millions, seduces people around the globe to join the voracious Western appetite for consumption, making thieves of ourselves and of others as well.

Clearly, context is important in understanding any experience, especially experiences with alleged ethical import. I have tried here to look at human experience and related moral thinking within a broad, indeed a global, context, beginning with Jared Diamond's sweeping account of human development from hunter-gatherer 13,000 years ago to nation-state citizen today. In both Diamond's geophysical account and in the market globalization of recent decades, ethics is hard to find. But in the outsider wisdom challenges to mainstream philosophical ethics, and in the critics of development, we see moral reasoning arising from lived experience sufficient to keep asking the question, "How are we to live?" and to continue finding it both important and difficult to answer. The critics have kept alive the notion of human development as having to do with more than per capita annual income, as having to do, rather, with human fulfillment. Various expressions of collective wisdom on how life should be lived continue to challenge dominant values.

Within this consideration of experiential aspects of ethical thought, we distinguished experiencing directly in our own life encounters from experiencing indirectly, through the expressions of others, whether those expressions be in conventional language or a nondiscursive articulate form, like art, music, or film. Along the way, we set aside considerations of ethical import arising from such indirect experiences. It is to these that we now turn.

NOTES

1. Diamond, Jerod, *Guns, Germs and Steel: The Fates of Human Societies* (New York: W. W. Norton, 1998).

2. Campbell, Joseph, *The Power of Myth* (New York: Doubleday, 1988), 31–32.

3. Campbell, *The Power of Myth*, 39.

4. Campbell, *The Power of Myth*, 32.

5. DuBois, W.E.B., *The Souls of Black Folk* (New York: Bantam Books, 1989; originally published in 1903), 3.

6. hooks, bell, *Feminist Theory: From Margin to Center* (Boston: South End Press, 1984), 10.

7. Frye, Marilyn, *The Politics of Reality: Essays in Feminist Theory* (Trumansburg, NY: The Crossing Press, 1983), 17.

8. Chisholm, Roderick M., *Person and Object* (La Salle, IL: Open Court, 1976), 16, emphasis in the original.

9. Truman, Harry S., Inaugural Address, quoted in Esteva, Gustavo, "Development," in *The Development Dictionary* (London, UK: Zed Books, 1992), 6.

10. Esteva, "Development," 7.

11. Sachs, Wolfgang, "One World," in *The Development Dictionary*, 104.

12. "Net Transfer of Financial Resources to Developing Countries, 1993–2000," UN/DESA, based on International Monetary Fund, *World Economic Outlook*, May, 2001.

13. Sachs, Wolfgang, "Introduction," in *The Development Dictionary*, 2.

14. West, Cornel, *Race Matters* (Boston: Beacon Press, 1993), 17.

15. Sachs, "One World," 102.

16. Sachs, "One World."

17. Sachs, "One World," 104.

18. Illich, Ivan, "Twenty-Six Years Later: Ivan Illich in Conversation with Majid Rahnema," in *The Post Development Reader*, ed. Majid Rahnema (London, UK: Zed Books, 1997), 109.

19. Gandhi, Mohandas K., "The Quest for Simplicity: My Idea of Swaraj," in *The Post Development Reader*, 307.

Chapter Four

Aesthetic Aspects of
Ethical Thought

In order to understand the aesthetic in its ultimate and approved forms, one
must begin with it in the raw; in the events and senses that hold the atten-
tive eye and ear.

—John Dewey

"Aesthetic," from the Greek, *aisthetikos*, means perception or perceptive.
Most English speakers are more familiar with "anaesthetic," the opposite notion, that which dulls perception or renders us unperceptive, leaving us without usual abilities to perceive. In English, aesthetic has come to mean not so
much the ordinary capacity for sensation but a special sort of sensing, a sensitivity to savoring or holding on to perceptions for themselves rather than going past them to something else outside the sensation. For example, we might
enjoy a picture simply for the sensing of it, the sheer value of looking at it for
its shapes, colors, textures, dramatic qualities, and the way it animates our
imaginations. That is very different from using the picture as we use a map,
viewing it to get information about what it depicts, using it to bring outside
facts to mind rather than savoring the meaning and form of the picture itself.
We can have aesthetic experience of things and scenes in nature, like trees or
sunsets, and of ordinary objects around us, like pencils and desks, or aesthetic
experiences can be stimulated by works of art, things created with the deliberate hope of engaging and satisfying our aesthetic sensitivities. Often aesthetic
experiences are described as having a rightness about them that cannot quite
be put into words, although many theorists have used millions of words trying.
Some aestheticians suggest that works of art are made *because* conventional
language is inadequate to express what the work expresses in a different

medium, be it painting, dance, sculpture, poetry, music, film, or another art form. This is one way of explaining why art is found in all cultures.

Aristotle's *Poetics* is one of the earliest and most influential discussions of aesthetics in the Western tradition. *Poesis* means making, and the book opens with a preliminary consideration of principles that Aristotle uses to explain the human capacity for making things to express ourselves. He begins by recognizing *mimesis*, imitation, as a common human practice, and suggests that the arts generally can be understood as various forms of imitation, by means of color and shape, voice, gesture, language, melody, rhythm, and action. Aristotle speculates that the desire to imitate is natural to humans, and he suggests that imitations enable humans to gain their earliest knowledge, in part because of "universal enjoyment in imitations." For Aristotle, "learning is the most pleasant of all experiences, not only for philosophers but for the rest of mankind as well."[1] Much of our learning comes from imitating others, or from imitations that express the insights of others. As we noted in referring to his ethics above, imitation and experience are central to Aristotle's outlook, so we find them at the heart of his aesthetics as well, shaping our views, making us who we are. The aesthetic is linked both to enjoyment of perceptual experiences and to learning through imitation; we take delight first in the perceptions themselves as they capture our attention and animate our imagination and our second delight is in learning through such enjoyable perceiving.

Dominant moral theory has tended to prefer Kant to Aristotle regarding the role of experience in ethical thought. The same preference is apparent concerning the relationships of aesthetics and imitation to ethics. Whereas Aristotle treats truth, goodness, and beauty as interrelated notions, Kant keeps them distinct from one another, treating each in a separate book.[2] Underscoring this separation, Kant famously claims, "worse service cannot be rendered morality than an attempt be made to derive it from examples" arguing that "every example of morality presented . . . must first be judged according to principles of morality in order to see whether it is fit to serve as an original example."[3] Kant insists on his narrower, more scientific notion of reason as opposed to Aristotle's broad view of experience for our source of values, saying, contrary to Aristotle, that "imitation has no place at all in moral matters."[4] Yet common sense—as well as prevailing judgment in contemporary education and psychology—seems to be with Aristotle on imitation, emphasizing the importance of practice in matters of value. We are enormously influenced in our value formation by the home life, community, role models, and culture of our upbringing, that is, by the way of life we have lived. The tension between Kant and Aristotle on experience offers another instance of the problem of the criterion: while Kant may want a single and universal moral criterion formed by reason a priori, that is, independently of experience, in fact our moral criteria are in constant give-and-take relationships with examples in experience, examples measured against the criteria and the criteria measured against examples. If our moral views require acts we find abhorrent or prohibit acts we find necessary, we sort out the dissonance as best we can, act, and construct as plausible an explanation as possible along the way, with our values guiding our actions *and* our experience informing and correcting our values as we go.

Aristotle goes on to underscore the influence of the aesthetic on the emotions in his explanation of tragedy, "an imitation, through action rather than narration, of a serious, complete and ample action, by means of language rendered pleasant at different places in the constituent parts by each of the aids [used to make the language more delightful], in which imitation there is also effected through pity and fear its catharsis of these and similar emotions."[5] Catharsis, the purgation and relief of emotion by bringing it to the surface of awareness, connects imitation, sensation, emotion, and intellect in Aristotle. Some experiences hit us in particularly powerful ways, forcing us to engage them emotionally and intellectually as well as perceptually. We come away from them changed by their impact because they reach us deeply. For Aristotle, Greek tragedies such as *Oedipus Rex*, had this affect and serve as his examples; for us, other experiences may prompt our feeling profoundly moved and even changed. Sometimes novels, plays, or films can have an influence as great or even greater than direct lived experiences, affecting us deeply, bringing emotions to awareness for reflection, suggesting clarity for coping with issues, even altering the course of life. While theorists debate the merits of catharsis as a measure of aesthetic value, Aristotle's insight of interest here is that things made, "imitations," can affect us profoundly through the experiencing of them, as can immediate experiences. Aesthetic experiences contribute to who we are by engaging, challenging, tempting, threatening, and gratifying us, and more.

In *Art as Experience*, John Dewey notes an important feature of experience akin to Aristotle's insights when he distinguishes the inchoate blur of typical experience from what he calls having *an* experience. In the case of *an* experience, something about the encounter grabs our attention, holds it, and we later organize our reflections around it. Such instances of experience stand out from the rushing process of sights, sounds, and smells constantly swimming around us, offering a sense of unity that can reestablish our equilibrium with our surroundings, providing points of reference as we construct accounts of our lives. In Dewey's words,

we have *an* experience when the material experienced runs its course to fulfillment. Then and only then is it integrated within and demarcated in the general

stream of experience from other experiences. A piece of work is finished in a
way that is satisfactory; a problem receives its solution; a game is played
through; a situation, whether that of eating a meal, playing a game of chess, car-
rying on a conversation, writing a book, or taking part in a political campaign,
is so rounded out that its close is a consummation and not a cessation. Such an
experience is a whole and carries with it its own individualizing quality and self-
sufficiency. It is *an* experience.[6]

Having *an* experience gives us the content about which we think. Dewey
goes on to understand works of art as expressions of features, moments, or aspects of experience that may have caught artists' imaginations, or that artists
may make to catch our attention and imagination, or both. His goal is "re-
covering the continuity of aesthetic experience with normal processes of living," noting the role of the aesthetic in helping us to inner harmony through
coming to terms with our environment.[7]

When I speak of the *aesthetic* here, I have in mind a very wide notion including but not limited to our savoring reactions to works of art. Aesthetic aspects of moral thought certainly include the arts widely conceived, but they
include these notions of perception identified by Aristotle and Dewey as well,
perceptions that grab our attention and hold it, which stand out from the blur
of impressions making up our lives, experiences engaging our consciousness,
attracting or repelling us intellectually and emotionally, providing points of
reference for our accounts of life, sometimes drawing cathartic reactions from
us. Here, aesthetic refers to such attention-holding experiences, whether they
involve works of art, phenomena in nature, aspects of culture, or things made
for purposes other than provoking aesthetic experiences.

While considering the role of experience in ethical thought in the previous
chapter, we focused on direct or immediate experience, the events each of us
live through. Along the way, we set aside experience that can be called indirect, experience we gain through reports from others by engaging their expressed accounts. We access experience indirectly through historical documents, news media, conversations, advertising, reports from witnesses, and
the like, but also through film, music, fiction, the various arts, and more. Any
experience, direct or indirect, may have ethical import, that is, it may contribute to our moral thought. Here we look at aesthetic aspects of experience
and at how aesthetic experience can influence moral vision.

To look at an injured, diseased, or emaciated child is to sense something
wrong. Regardless of our moral framework, whether we organize our moral
judgments around rights or consequences or duties or care or character, the
sight of a child hurt, sick, or malnourished gives rise to a sense of wrong
which often moves us to do something in an attempt to set things right. Organizations sometimes use powerful *images* to take advantage of just this sort

of expected reaction, to motivate charitable gifts for example. This is so common that people sometimes get hardened to such images, to insulate themselves from the feelings that the images stir. The point is that a simple image, as well as a sight in personal experience, can have significant emotional, intellectual, and moral import. This can work to stimulate positive moral feelings as well as negative, through the sight of, or an image of, a healthy, smiling child, for example. Often we check such experiential encounters against our values, sometimes to critique moral frameworks, or to refine moral criteria for consistency, bringing our rules and principles in line with experience. This can work in reverse as well, where moral convictions are so strong that the experiential encounter is called into question and reinterpreted to eliminate incompatibility with values.

There are important differences between the sight and the image, between actually seeing a starving child and seeing a photograph or a painting of one, or even conjuring the image in the imagination with the help of poetry, prose, or an eyewitness account. An image is a sight that is detached from the place and time it was created, and the selection and detachment implies a way of seeing.[8] A sight itself is necessarily attached to its context, although it can be misunderstood nonetheless. All of us with normal vision are accustomed to the sights of our usual surroundings, comfortable with their familiarity, but we bring more than normal eyesight to the experience; we bring a way of seeing as well, and part of our way of seeing is our moral vision, the values shaping our perspective. Many of our daily sights provoke aesthetic responses in us, and we find ourselves savoring the look of something, or repulsed by it, or a host of other reactions. This sort of aesthetic experience is a normal part of living our lives. In modern Western cultures, perhaps especially in American culture, experiencing art has been set apart from more ordinary experience in such a way that many people find art intimidating. The common expression, "I don't know anything about art, but I know what I like" conveys both the ordinariness of aesthetic perception, even though we rarely call it that, and, at the same time, a deference to art that suggests that many find it intimidating. Many people are quick to concede a kind of distance, alienation, even ignorance about art, unsure of how they are supposed to react to it. Here, I am interested both in our ordinary aesthetic experiences arising independently of art, and in our experiences with, and distance from, art. In both cases, I have a particular interest in ethical import.

Part of the distance many feel from art is due to our realization that, unlike the perceptions of daily experience, works of art and the selection and detachment they imply, are expressions of those who made them. And like linguistic expressions, they seem to convey meaning, yet not of the sort usually understood through social conventions or rules, the way languages convey meaning. Like linguistic expressions, artistic expressions imply meaning, but unlike language, works of art come at us without a conventional decoder system, leaving many of us puzzled about what to make of them. Nonetheless, they have their impact, often attracting and holding our attention, touching our intellect or emotions, moving us to question or reflect, or not; sometimes they leave us cold, or repulsed, or indifferent. Conceived widely, the arts can include much in the various media of mass communication, elements of popular culture broadcast on television, radio, film, magazines, and the Internet, much of it leaving various impressions on us whether we attend to them seriously or not. If we are confused, no doubt part of the puzzlement is prompted by a wish for clarity and for a reliable and straightforward means of interpretation, especially in the case of more serious, difficult, and challenging art. Yet, much of art defies easy translation from the various art media into conventional language; as noted above, Susanne Langer and other aesthetic theorists take this to be a distinguishing feature of art, that whatever a work expresses cannot be adequately expressed in conventional linguistic terms. Often, the whole point of artistic expression is to convey meaning in nondiscursive yet articulate forms.

It is here that art and morality are akin to one another. While ethical theorists attempt to capture moral meaning in rules, principles, necessary and sufficient conditions, formulas for right and wrong, and the like, moral dilemmas—and moral conflicts—often leave sensitive people struggling to act ethically even though there may not be applicable rules, or where there may be conflicting rules, or where ethical action may involve breaking rules, or stretching social conventions, or somehow accommodating competing conventions, even across cultures. Thinking about the tension between moral conventions and moral behavior reminds me of John Irving's novel, *The Cider House Rules*, which presents a plethora of situations wherein doing the right thing requires bending and breaking moral rules, somehow making the implausible plausible. In his novel, Irving provokes moral reflection of a critical sort that can confuse as well as deepen a reader's thinking. Irving is providing a context for readers to think about the problem of the criterion as it manifests itself in the moral lives of his characters, vividly depicting a series of struggles between moral criteria and situations in which thoughtful individuals suffer the dissonance brought on by tension between criteria and events, characters pushed to forge ethical actions incommensurate with social conventions. One of the hard lessons of life is realizing that many moral issues are not easily resolved, despite the supposed clarity and insistence of conventional morality.

At one point in *The Birth of Tragedy*, Nietzsche describes Hamlet as having looked truly into the essence of things and having thus gained knowledge so sickening that it has a paralyzing effect, a paradigm case of suffering the dissonant tension between one's moral framework and events. Rejecting a common interpretation of Hamlet as unsure of what to do in the face of his father's murder, Nietzsche insists that "knowledge kills action . . . not that cheap wisdom of Jack the Dreamer who reflects too much and, as it were, from an excess of possibilities does not get around to action." Nietzsche's Hamlet understands that his action could not change anything, and he finds it ridiculous and humiliating to "be asked to set right a world that is out of joint." Insight into the horrible truth sickens him to inaction.[9] This is suffering dissonance between values and events in the extreme, prompting moral skepticism. Nietzsche suggests what he takes to be the source of Hamlet's numbing incapacity, and in doing so Nietzsche is pointing to exactly what so many artists and theorists of art have said about art: that it can express what cannot be said in conventional language, that it offers forms of meaning that we do not yet know how to express discursively. Just as myths express collective wisdom, give form to experience, and help guide members of a culture through the challenges of life while heightening their awareness of being alive, so, too, works of art can provide moorings and sign posts along the way. The arts and the aesthetic can have significant impact on moral vision. Perhaps this impact is especially apparent when the dissonance between moral criteria and events is greatest.

If being ethical is not merely making derivations within ethical frameworks but acting deliberately, creatively, and even morally despite a poor fit between moral guidelines and events at hand, then aesthetic sense may be crucial to morality since our moral problems sometimes defy conventional ethical criteria. Besides, as Iris Murdoch has warned, moral differences are not always differences of choice, given the same facts, but can involve differences of moral vision.[10] It seems clear that while conventional reason makes derivations within moral frameworks from given criteria, conventional reason does not account for the particular moral vision within which it works, and it also seems clear that aesthetic factors can have significant influence on moral vision. As we have seen above, conceptions of reason vary widely, from a more restrictive modeling after textbook natural science to a more inclusive notion involving life-experience, emotion, and aesthetic dimensions. What we need is a sense of the aesthetic that somehow avoids the arbitrariness and thoroughgoing relativism so often associated with it.

In his characterization of the aesthetic, Dewey insists that "the esthetic cannot be marked off from intellectual experience since the latter must bear an esthetic stamp to be itself complete."[11] This is reminiscent of his fellow pragmatists C. S. Peirce and William James who both note an aesthetic sense of clarity and wholeness as indicative of satisfying curiosity and settling belief. Dewey anchors his sense of the aesthetic in the ancient Greek identification of good conduct having proportion, grace, and harmony, where beauty and goodness are inseparable. For Dewey, "the non-esthetic lies within two limits. At one pole is the loose succession that does not begin at any particular place and that ends—in the sense of ceasing—at no particular place. At the other pole is arrest, constriction, proceeding from parts having only a mechanical connection."[12] So much ordinary experience falls under one or the other of these descriptions that they come to be taken as norms for all experience. "Then, when the esthetic appears, it so sharply contrasts with the picture that has been formed of experience that . . . the esthetic is given an outside place and status." Dewey counters this separation of the aesthetic by suggesting that "no experience of whatever sort is a unity unless it has esthetic quality."[13]

For Dewey, the opposite of the aesthetic is the arbitrary and a routine submission to conventional practices and procedures. "Rigid abstinence, coerced submission, tightness on one side and dissipation, incoherence and aimless indulgence on the other, are deviations in opposite directions from the unity of *an* experience."[14] He sees his aesthetic as akin to Aristotle's notion of virtue as a state of character by which an intelligent person finds a mean between the vices of excess and deficiency, as courage is at a mean between cowardice and recklessness for example. For Aristotle, virtue or excellence of character, finds and chooses what is intermediate. Dewey's example is of a job interview. It may be mechanical, with a candidate's replies to set questions judged perfunctorily and with the job-appointment made or denied as a function of the answers. Or it may consist of an interplay between applicant and manager, involving emotions of hope or despair initially, and elation or disappointment at the close, the interview constituting *an* experience, a unified whole, ordered, and complete. The employer may appraise the character of the applicant by emotional reactions, may imaginatively project the candidate into the job, and may judge fitness for the appointment by the way attitude, gesture, words, and other elements of the scene harmonize or clash with the interviewer's vision of the position. Dewey's point is that there are inherently aesthetic aspects to every situation in which there are uncertainty and suspense, and that drama or fiction can provide a more accurate account of such experiences than can data reports.[15]

We can elaborate the kinship between ethics and aesthetics to which Dewey calls attention by considering the persistent clash, in Western ethical thought, between absolutism on the one hand and relativism on the other. While settling moral questions once and for all has been a longed-for ideal of many, increasing awareness of value diversity has eroded the absolutist effort and encouraged a rival advocacy for toleration, acceptance, and even celebration of difference. As the ranks of those applauding diversity and pluralism have grown, so the ranks of those expecting to justify universal and absolutist values have diminished, and their members have become increasingly defensive. Contemporary postmodern critiques as well as deconstructions of traditional and dominant values have widened the gap between absolutist and relativist value theorists. Traditionally, aesthetic judgment has been highly suspect, often identified with mere taste—about which there can be no meaningful disputes—while moral judgment, although too subjective and relative to have the status of scientific judgment, has been widely considered to be meaningful, certainly not reducible to mere taste. Put bluntly, from the perspective of conventional wisdom, aesthetics is thought to be relative and arbitrary, ethics to be approximate at best, and science to be approaching the absolute. Dewey's effort is to deny this neat separation by calling attention to aesthetic aspects of every judgment. Following his recognition of aesthetic dimensions of science and ethics suggests not so much solving the problem of the gap between absolutists and relativists as dissolving it. If every situation of uncertainty and suspense involves inherently aesthetic factors, then surely science and ethics have aesthetic aspects. If aesthetic judgment involves valuing unity, wholeness, completion, consummation, and fulfillment, then to dismiss aesthetic judgment as arbitrary is to misconceive and misunderstand it completely. Rather than encourage separation and opposition between science, ethics and aesthetics, Dewey sees them as integrated. This means that science is not nearly so absolute as typical science textbooks have it, that aesthetics is not nearly so arbitrary as conventional wisdom takes it to be, and that ethics is neither random nor absolute, despite claims of conflicting proponents, the skeptical and the dogmatic.

Let me offer a more concrete picture of the science/ethics/aesthetics kinship suggested above. Consider the notion of peace. Peace can be and often is conceived as the absence of war. In this conception, nations are at peace if they are not engaged in armed conflict, and their citizens are peaceful if they are orderly and law-abiding. I think of this as negative peace, not only because the definition itself is negative (that is, made by reference to what is *not* characteristic of the term in question), but also because of what this conception lacks. Positive peace would consist in cooperative behavior among citizens—or nations—that arises freely within the relevant group through uncoerced choice. Negative peace could be maintained by coercive force or threat of force from outside the group, by oppressive government officials or by occupying armies for example. So negative peace lacks the internally willed cooperation characteristic of positive peace.[16] These contrasting conceptions of peace can be used to illustrate Dewey's "enemies" of the aesthetic, with war at the pole of randomness and incoherence, and with negative peace at the pole of coerced submission and mechanical tightness.

Positive peace avoids these deviations and forms a unity, a whole ordered meaningfully and complete within itself rather than either disordered, or orderly by force from the outside. Dewey sees his sense of the aesthetic converging with Aristotle's notion of virtue as choice at a mean between excess and deficiency, and in the convergence is the aesthetic sense of the good—beautiful action—a union of moral and aesthetic thought. Surely genuine peace has this aesthetic quality that both war and negative peace lack. The scientific aspect completing the integration of science, aesthetics, and ethics lies in the empirically discovered and "experimentally" confirmed efficacy of nonviolent direct action characteristic of genuine peace.[17]

Just as the aesthetic unifies art and experience, so it unifies form and function as well, and in the process suggests a union of means and ends. "Early in the history of philosophic thought the value of shape in making possible the definition and classification of objects was noted and was seized upon."[18] As Dewey tells us, if the relationship of shape to use is ignored, then it is easy to follow the reasoning that led to the metaphysical theory in which forms are considered the essence of things. We typically distinguish objects perceived by their shapes. But form alone cannot account for things in experience; the empirical fact of the relationship of form to use is needed, in accounting for a spoon, for example, or a bodily organ. The aesthetic enters when form and function are integrated into a unified whole, separable only in abstract thought. We sense this immediately in architecture, interior design, pottery, clothing, landscape, and the like, when our attention is drawn to and held by forms which satisfy our aesthetic and practical senses creatively and simultaneously, forms that we find attractive and that enhance usefulness. The same sort of aesthetic unity is found between means and ends in ethics. As noted in the consideration of ethical frameworks above, traditional ethical thought, especially since the seventeenth century, has been dominated by duty-based or deontological ethics on the one hand, and results-based or consequentialist ethics on the other, or, as Nussbaum puts it, by Kant and Mill. This focus has pressed ethical theorists to take sides on whether morality is a matter of means, that is, of deference to certain obligations, or a matter of ends, that is, of achieving certain results. Is being moral simply doing our duty regardless of consequences? Is being moral simply gaining desired results regardless of how we do so? The aesthetic enters when means and ends coalesce. As Dewey puts it, "all the cases in which means and ends are external to one another are nonesthetic. This externality may even be regarded as a definition of the nonesthetic."[19] So the ends do not justify the means, nor vice versa.

Gandhi is particularly helpful in understanding this coalescence of ends and means: "The means may be likened to a seed, the end to a tree; and there is just the same inviolable connection between the means and the end as there is between the seed and the tree."[20] Planting acorns does not yield maples; dishonest judgment does not make science. This works in both directions. Results flow from the means adopted, and the nature of the ends in view restrict our choice of means to be undertaken. Gandhi elaborates the point with another example: "If I want to deprive you of your watch, I shall certainly have to fight for it; if I want to buy your watch, I shall have to pay for it; and if I want a gift, I shall have to plead for it; and, according to the means I employ, the watch is stolen property, my own property, or a donation."[21] The separation of means and ends, again, is only possible in the abstract. As noted above, being moral is not simply committing to an ethical framework and mechanically calculating derivative acts. The moral life involves a continuing reflective process of checking our means and ends against one another, testing our moral criteria against events in our lives, constantly questioning means and ends as well as criteria and experience, and continually adjusting for improved fit among them. This is why various experiences can provoke cognitive dissonance sufficient to shake our values to the core, especially when they involve collisions between cultures.

This discussion about the relationship between science, ethics, and aesthetics has included references to the ancient Greek union of the good, the true, and the beautiful, but to this point in reflecting on aesthetic aspects of ethical thought I have spoken mainly about the relationship of goodness to beauty. I mentioned in passing the modern inclination to separate rather than integrate the three concepts; the centrality of unity and completion in the notion of the aesthetic under consideration here requires reflection on truth as well. Philosophers have struggled for centuries with the notion of the true, and many competing theories of truth are articulated, debated, and defended across Western intellectual history, theories that we cannot survey here. Much of the discussion has involved identifying truth to be correct assertions about whatever is in fact the case. This has led to debates of a metaphysical sort: What exists? What is real? How do we know it? And at various points in the history of Western philosophy there have been claims about moral truth as existent and available for discovery. It is easy to see how such issues can be connected to the various ethical frameworks discussed above: Are rights invented or discovered? Are duties somehow reflective of natural moral law comparable to natural physical law? Is the greater good sought by utilitarians a natural reality, or culturally relative? Are notions of virtue tied to human nature, to culture, or grounded in another way? Is care something more than a relative cultural value? Clearly, the notion of truth has provided science with a foundational anchor that makes scientific aspirations for universality plausible. Do ethics and aesthetics need truth as well to avoid loss of meaning? Is meaning lost without universality? Certainly we cannot address all of these questions; they are included here to convey the importance of taking up the notion of truth and its relation to moral thought.

Etymologically, "truth" is derived from the Old English, *treowth*, which literally means having good faith. Truth shares its etymology with "troth," as in "betrothal" or "thereto I pledge thee my troth" in a wedding ceremony. The notion is that of a pledge, or giving one's word. So, truth turns out to be more closely tied with ethics and aesthetics than many might expect. And science turns out to be linked with ethics and aesthetics as well in that all three involve judgments, and the value of judgments depends on the good faith of those who make them. Dating from the earliest record of the notion, truth indicates a pledge or guarantee that the judgments to which it is ascribed are reliable, that you can take the word of the claimant, that assertions are made in good faith. What is especially interesting about this etymology is that, taken literally, truth does not necessitate wading into metaphysical theories on the nature of existence or debates about what it means to say something is real. Some theorists may choose to go that direction in their efforts to find justifications for their claims, but it is not necessary to do so. A scientist concerned about finding a helpful treatment for a particular disease need not get into metaphysics. A moralist focused on finding a resolution to a particular ethical conflict is concerned about what will satisfy contesting parties and promise a lasting agreement, not whether morality reflects ultimate reality. Those taking aesthetic judgment seriously need not appeal to metaphysics to express their perspectives meaningfully. But because science is broadly understood to ground its claims in facts and to project universal principles, and because science is widely taken to be *the* model of knowledge, ethics and aesthetics are expected to rest on facts to back up their claims and to issue universal statements as well. Nonetheless, as suggested above, science may not be as positivistic as often thought; besides, ethics and aesthetics may have other than metaphysical and epistemological objectives. Meaning is not exhausted by reference to empirical verifiability plus the definitions of relevant terms; meaning includes good faith, a sense of unity, fulfillment, and completion, as well as a healthy respect for lived experience, whether in science, ethics, or aesthetics.

Of course, good faith alone does not make for good science, nor does it make for good art or good ethics. Sincerity is necessary but not sufficient to meet the standards of these areas of thought. And although science, ethics, and aesthetics are interrelated, they are not identical. Each involves aspects of the others, but none can be eliminated by reduction to any of the others. Because natural science has been so successful for the past few hundred years, the rest of thought has been increasingly pressed to be more like science. This led to important advances in physical, empirical studies in many fields, but the price has been reduced emphasis on aesthetic and ethical dimensions of thought, to the point that they are increasingly ignored and even denied meaning. As Charles Taylor has pointed out, "modern philosophy, and to some extent modern culture, has lost its grip on the proper patterns of practical reason. Moral argument is understood according to inappropriate models, and this naturally leads to skepticism and despair, which in turn has an effect on our conception of morality, gives it a new shape (or misshapes it)."[22] But foundationalist grounding is only one sort of reasoning. Rational accounts are not limited to explanation by subsumption under criteria; reasoning also includes comparative judgments, critical tests for coherence, as well as articulation for clarity, and more.[23] The whole point of addressing ethical and aesthetic dimensions of life here is to call attention to their significance, to underscore their contributions to what Aristotle called "living well," including, but not limited to, their contributions to science.

There is another similarity between science, ethics, and aesthetics that merits attention. It is the relative certainty that can be achieved in the negative case by comparison with the tentative endorsement of the positive. In the logic of empirical science, hypotheses can be defeated with certainty but their confirmation is probable at best. As Popper puts it, much of science amounts to trial and error-elimination, or conjecture and refutation. In a strikingly similar way, ethics achieves broad agreement on what is wrong or evil, what must be avoided—violence, torture, aggression, theft, and the like—but has more limited success getting to consensus on what is right and good. Even in aesthetics, it seems plausible to suggest that it is easier to get agreement about the unaesthetic or ugly, or about what constitutes bad art, than to achieve consensus on beauty or good art. The true, the good, and the beautiful are elusive ideals to which many aspire, but we rarely have the confidence to claim having captured them once and for all. But falsehood, evil, and ugliness seem less out of reach, easier to confirm, more amenable to agreement. This is reminiscent of Socratic wisdom, Socrates' knowing that he does not know, an epistemologically respectable position in which to find ourselves. Regarding values, Socrates cites his *daimon* or inner voice, which never tells him what to do but always guides him away from wrong action.

Conceiving rationality as consisting, at least in part, of diverse human efforts to understand and express goodness, truth, and beauty opens awareness to aspects of aesthetics, ethics, and science each entangled in the others. Avoiding the neat but artificial separation of these aspects of thought respects thinking as the rich, complex, diverse, and, borrowing Walzer's term, "thick"[24] phenomenon that it is and saves us from the oversimplifications of reductionism. Such an integrated notion of thought leaves room for nondiscursive articulate form as well as for conventional language and traditional proof systems. Even the unsayable can be expressed, by way of gesture, outcry, music, visual image, dance, poem, and other media, whatever can animate our imaginations and provide expressions for our consideration. This offers hope for broadening and deepening understanding across the many barriers of conventional expression. Paul Gilroy suggests that it can even be used to "challenge the privileged conceptions of both language and writing as preeminent expressions of human consciousness,"[25] a necessary step in opening awareness to illiterate and otherwise silenced "others," those in dominant as well as subordinate cultures who remain outsiders to first-world conventional wisdom.

Led by this characterization of the aesthetic drawn from Aristotle, Langer, Dewey, and Gilroy, we can now turn to a consideration of metaphor and its role in moral vision.

NOTES

1. Aristotle, *The Poetics*, tr. Preston H. Epps (Chapel Hill: The University of North Carolina Press, 1942), 6.

2. *The Critique of Pure Reason* (truth), *The Critique of Practical Reason* (goodness), and *The Critique of Judgment* (beauty).

3. Kant, Immanuel, *Grounding of the Metaphysics of Morals* (1785), tr. James W. Ellington (Indianapolis: Hackett Publishing Company, 1981), 20.

4. Kant, *Grounding of the Metaphysics of Morals*, 21.

5. Kant, *Grounding of the Metaphysics of Morals*, 11.

6. Dewey, John, *Art as Experience* (New York: Capricorn Books, 1958), 35.

7. Dewey, *Art as Experience*, 10, 17.

8. Berger, John, *Ways of Seeing* (London, UK: British Broadcasting Corporation and Penguin Books, 1972), 9–10.

9. Nietzsche, Friedrich, *The Birth of Tragedy* (1872), tr. Walter Kaufmann (New York: Vintage Books, 1967), 60.

10. Murdoch, Iris, "Vision and Choice in Morality," *Proceedings of the Aristotelian Society*, 1956, in *Christian Ethics and Contemporary Philosophy*, ed. Ian Ramsey (New York: Macmillan Co., 1966), 40.

11. Dewey, *Art as Experience*, 38.

12. Dewey, *Art as Experience*, 40.

13. Dewey, *Art as Experience*, 40.

14. Dewey, *Art as Experience*, 40.

15. Dewey, *Art as Experience*, 43.

16. Cady, Duane L., *From Warism to Pacifism: A Moral Continuum* (Philadelphia: Temple University Press, 1989). See chapter 5: "Positive Peace," 77–93.

17. See Sharp, Gene, *Power and Struggle*, Part One of *The Politics of Nonviolent Action* (Boston: Porter Sargent, 1973) and Gandhi, Mohandas K., *An Autobiography: The Story of My Experiments with Truth* (Boston: Beacon Press, 1957).

18. Dewey, *Art as Experience*, 115.

19. Dewey, *Art as Experience*, 198.

20. Gandhi, Mohandas K., "Means and Ends" in *Nonviolent Resistance*, ed. Bharatan Kumarappa (New York: Schocken Books, 1961), 10.

21. Gandhi, "Means and Ends," 11.

22. Taylor, Charles, "Explanation and Practical Reason," in *The Quality of Life*, eds. Martha C. Nussbaum and Amartya Sen (Oxford, UK: Clarendon Press, 1993), 230.

23. Taylor, "Explanation and Practical Reason," 230.

24. Walzer, Michael, "Objectivity and Social Meaning," in *The Quality of Life*, 165–77.

25. Gilroy, Paul, *The Black Atlantic* (Cambridge, MA: Harvard University Press, 1993), 74.

Chapter Five

Morals and Metaphors

Metaphors are windows that require an act of the synthetic imagination.

—Deane Curtin

Metaphor is an ancient Greek word referring to an expression that transfers meaning from a literal to a figurative form. For example, "ghetto" is commonly used to refer to a section of an American city with a high concentration of both black people and poverty. But such areas are not literally ghettos. In its literal use, ghetto refers to the quarter of an eastern European city, from the seventeenth and into the twentieth centuries, to which Jews were confined. Ghettos were walled, gated, sometimes locked areas in which Jews had their homes and to which they had to return from work or business; their movement about the city was not free. With the rise of the Nazi party in Germany in the 1930s, ghettos became more like prisons. It was probably in the 1940s that someone created the ghetto metaphor that has become so common that some younger readers may have taken it as the literal meaning when they first learned its meaning. It is a powerful metaphor, one that challenges policies and values by suggesting that dominant society does not allow freedom to poor black people, but deliberately confines them because they are poor and black. The expression is so widely used that it has become nearly literal and no longer requires the leap of imaginative connection and insight that the early use of the metaphor demanded.

Metaphors can also be expressed in nonlinguistic forms. Visual metaphors are common in political cartooning; for example, to draw President Lyndon Johnson as Shakespeare's King Lear and to do so during the war in Vietnam was a way of provoking readers to see the war as Johnson's tragedy. Visual metaphors are frequently used in drama, film, painting, and other graphic arts, as well as in advertising. Musical metaphors transfer the meaning of a conventional musical expression to a figurative one, as when a sacred melody is inserted in a political medley, or vice versa, sometimes for comic effect or to make a critical point, at others to stretch the imaginations of listeners, to provoke thought beyond the anticipated subject. In every case, understanding a metaphor requires understanding two contexts and making a connection between them. A metaphor is like an argument with a necessary piece missing, the part through which the thinking is mediated, the piece that links the two meanings that are tied metaphorically. Metaphors are especially powerful contributors to reasoning because they suggest the missing connection and they require thoughtful participation from those who would understand them, in order to discover the meaning link.[1]

Susanne Langer connects metaphor to abstraction. Rivers and rumors may *run* through town; both metaphors may have been inspired by the running of people, which may help explain the metaphors of a fence running along the road, a politician running for office, and a car running in the garage. Yet neither rivers, rumors, fences, politicians, nor automobiles bring to mind the speedy leg action of sprinters. The constant figurative use of "run" has made it a faded metaphor and generalized its sense so that the various specific senses emerge only in their separate contexts. For Langer, "every new experience, or new idea about things, evokes first of all some metaphorical expression. As the idea becomes familiar, this expression fades to a new literal use, . . . a more general use." Encountering the limits of language, having thoughts beyond what we can express in available words, leads us to metaphorical expression. "Metaphor is our most striking evidence of *abstractive seeing*, of the power of human minds to use presentational symbols."[2]

In this view, taking scientific language as the model on which to base other forms of expression is actually backwards, because scientific expression is itself based on faded metaphors. Art, ethics, myth, and other forms of expression are not just sloppy science; they are symbolic transformations ahead of the regularity of usage that comes with metaphors fading into the literal meanings of conventional discourse, eventually making scientific talk possible. "Technical advances make demands on our language which are met by the elaboration of mathematical, logical, and scientific terminologies." With repeated use, the meanings of words gain precision, and "speech becomes increasingly discursive, practical, prosaic, until human beings can actually believe that it was invented as a utility, and was later embellished with metaphors,"[3] even when language development actually works the other way around, with figurative expressions well ahead of conventional meaning. Metaphor turns out to be the basis for the growth of thought. Insight, itself a metaphor for rational recognition, connects two things not previously connected, by means of a word, image, or other expression, and if the connection sticks, that is, if the relationship drawn between two contexts proves meaningful and the expression gains usage, then the metaphor is on its way to fading into literal use. For Langer, imaginative connections of thought expressed metaphorically are the steps that lead human development. Dance, ritual, myth, music, drama, visual arts, social activism, ethics, and science all are outgrowths of this process of symbolic transformation.

Imagining is a central feature of any thought. Envisioning the world as a realm of living forces—the powers of the sea, of the heavens, of spirits—is a metaphor, an expression of a connection between ourselves, our experiences, fears, and hopes, and the world in which we live. To see the world as somehow enchanted is to be oriented by way of a very different metaphor, and consequently to live in a very different world, rather than seeing the world as matter and only matter, where everything we know and love is reducible to physical elements. For one, the world is alive; for the other, it is a mechanism. The point here is not to advocate for any particular conceptual world nor to suggest that every conceptual world is as valuable as every other. Rather, the point is to highlight the centrality of metaphor in understanding perspective. If Langer is on to something with her notion that we use metaphors to stretch expression beyond what can be said conventionally and that repeated use of metaphors fades them into literal use, creating general terms and thus both growing conventional language and allowing increased abstraction, then we might try to explain the gap between ethical criteria and moral life by means of her analysis.

Extending Langer's reasoning on the role of metaphor in language development to the problem of the criterion in ethics suggests that functioning within a particular moral vision leads to repeated use of metaphors, their fading into conventional use, fostering general terms, increasing articulation and precision, and eventually settling into moral criteria that are progressively systematic, explicit, rule oriented, and clear. Moral reasoning can be rigorous and modeled after science, where derivations can be made and proof-like arguments offered. This is what happens *within* a Kantian framework or *within* Mill's rule utilitarianism. The process is the same as the one in the history of science to which Thomas Kuhn calls our attention in *The Structure of Scientific Revolutions*, where widely recognized scientific achievements are taken as models for practice by a community of scientists. Normal science is the "strenuous and devoted attempt to force nature into the conceptual boxes supplied by professional education. . . . Normal science, the activity in which most scientists inevitably spend almost all their time, is predicated on the assumption that the scientific community knows what the world is like."[4] The same could be said for normal ethics. Across history, normal science—and normal ethics—periodically go astray or exhaust the explanatory value of the dominant traditions. This brings investigations that ultimately lead to new commitments, to different bases for professional practices, to what Kuhn calls paradigm shifts. Progress is not the smooth, cumulative, linear growth that textbooks lead us to imagine, but instead it is a series of creative bursts followed by careful, sometimes tedious working-out of implications suggested by a given paradigm. The critiques of Enlightenment Liberalism offered by MacIntyre and Rorty, and the alternative directions for value theory suggested by Murdoch, Langer, Nussbaum, Gilroy, and others may indicate exhaustion of a tradition and new possibilities for where ethics might go. Perhaps the rise of feminist action and subsequent feminist philosophy, racial equality activism and subsequent civil rights theorizing, and nonviolence movements and subsequent systematizing and articulation of nonviolence theory all suggest a significant pattern in moral history of visionary moral practice running out ahead of traditional and conventional ethical thought. Theorists then "mop-up" (to borrow Kuhn's term) by systematizing and making precise the implications of the visionary practice, casting them in criteria, rules, and principles.

Clearly, systematic and proof-like reasoning go on *within* dominant value traditions. But it seems less effective in resolving issues *between* them. Perhaps this is because being within a value tradition, holding a particular moral vision, engaging experience through the perspective of a moral framework, is not itself a result of derivative reasoning but is more like the reasoning involved in making, or in grasping, a metaphor. Just as working within a particular scientific paradigm orients each scientist to the work—what constitutes a problem, what constitutes a solution, what counts as evidence, and so on—perhaps adopting a moral vision orients individuals to moral life, setting forth structures within which one can reason derivatively. Given the role and power of metaphor in stretching thought beyond what can be said explicitly in conventional terms, we need to look at how metaphors function in our moral lives.[5]

Moral leaders have always used metaphors to capture the attention and imagination of those who come to follow their lead. Because metaphors stretch thought beyond what can be articulated conventionally and also require an active leap of thought from literal to figurative meaning in the minds of those engaging them, metaphors are especially well suited to moral visionaries in their efforts to inspire action from others. Gandhi's decision to abandon Western dress and adopt simple clothing of home-spun fabric created a visual metaphor that projected his political message with every encounter, whether in media images or in person. For Gandhi, a better future for India was not to be had by following "advanced" British ways but by empowering the masses to take responsibility for the rule of their own nation.

Through the simple act of dressing each day, Gandhi could simultaneously identify with the Indian masses and reject any acknowledgment of the superiority of British culture. The image of an Oxford-educated political revolutionary dressing like the Indian masses, at times sitting and spinning cotton during discussions of national independence, said more to his nation, the British, and the world than his explicit political analysis could say.

Martin Luther King, Jr., did something similar in Birmingham in 1963 when the city leaders and those demonstrating for desegregated lunch counters were deadlocked, hundreds of demonstrators jailed, and negotiations stalled. At a loss for how to break the standoff, Dr. King put on a work shirt and blue jeans, allowed himself to be arrested, and went into jail alongside the ordinary black folks of Birmingham who had stood with him against racial segregation. While sitting in jail, King responded to a published statement by eight Alabama clergy criticizing him and the Southern Christian Leadership Conference (SCLC) for their "unwise and untimely" actions. King's reply was his "Letter from Birmingham Jail," but the act of solidarity with demonstrators, and the media images of police dogs and fire hoses being used on black children-demonstrators, broadcast worldwide, spoke as powerfully as his text.[6] The SCLC used a version of Gandhi's metaphor again after King's murder, during the poor people's campaign in Washington, D.C., when King's simple coffin was carried on a buckboard and pulled through the city by a mule, again identifying the civil rights movement with the black working-poor more powerfully than words could convey.

Moral metaphors need not be executed with such grand strokes. They can be effective explanatory tools even in modest settings and uses. In teaching ethics, I have frequently found students more responsive to metaphoric expressions of moral positions than to explicit accounts from course readings. My colleagues confirm that attracting, engaging, and holding students' attention on ethical theory is enhanced by pedagogical metaphors, and many theorists make use of metaphors in their explicit accounts. This is especially common in ancient texts. Stripping metaphors from Plato would vacate his dialogues of much of his most powerful imagery—desire as a leaky jar that can never be filled; the three-part self—rational, emotional, and physical—as a charioteer, struggling with a team of horses; the state as a ship, in need of captain and sailors; Socrates as a midwife delivering thoughts; the mind as an aviary; death as dreamless sleep; death as escape; death as a journey; and so on. Contemporary thinkers also use powerful metaphors to capture moral imagination. W.E.B. DuBois's use of the veil metaphor to express his sense of the American racial divide is a classic case. More recently, Garrett Hardin put a lifeboat metaphor to effective use in discussing global supply and demand and problems of scarcity. And Marilyn Frye's birdcage imagery for oppression of women has helped a generation of students grasp the way multiple minor barriers, each by itself a mere annoyance, can work together to create sexist restriction and entrapment. Metaphors are not only effective and engaging pedagogical devices, they also stretch thinking and actively involve those trying to understand them.

Often conventional ethical thought is metaphor driven. People who envision life to be a gift make very different moral choices than those who see life as a test. Perhaps this is the sort of thing Iris Murdoch has in mind when she says that moral differences can be more differences of vision than differences of choice.[7] In the gift metaphor, gratitude is a central orientation, often reflected in a commitment to respect and preserve life. Seeing life as a test orients one to being judged and to judging, and consequently to expectations of reward or punishment and perhaps to meting out punishments and rewards to others, reinforcing the norms against which the test is judged. The differences between the decisions made from within each of these metaphors are more the function of differences in vision than due to different choices, since the choices flow rather naturally from within the vision, which acts like a conceptual framework, structuring what fits, what follows, what makes sense, as well as establishing what is out of the question, beyond consideration, even nonsensical. Functioning from within a particular moral vision, in this case what can be called a life metaphor, is like putting on a set of lenses through which the moral world is seen, defined, interpreted, and understood. Metaphors are especially powerful expressions of moral perspective because they can project more than can be said explicitly, they orient subsequent moral thought in their terms, and they attract, engage, animate, and hold the attention of those who embrace them.

Conventional morality seems to reflect dozens of moral visions that might be described by reference to what I am calling life metaphors. Many people seem to be oriented to the world from within the vision of life as war, where battle is the predominant means and winning is the goal, the prize for prevailing in a lifelong series of conflicts. Sometimes winning is personal, sometimes institutional, but always the winning itself rather than the spoils of victory is the end in view. Others may be operating through a vision of life as a market, with gain as the purpose and dealing as the mechanism for achievement. In this view, everything comes down to a "bottom line," which is usually calculated through a cost/benefit analysis. Conceiving of life as a journey is so common that the metaphoric expression has become a cliché, a fading metaphor that has given rise to its own offshoots as people speak of spiritual journeys, relationship journeys, career journeys, and so on. In each case, the metaphor structures values around a theme of expecting and accepting change, of adventure, and of curiosity and perhaps toleration. To some, life is a puzzle, a question, a problem to be solved. This orientation is characterized by a persistent search for meaning through intellectual examination. Envisioning life as an art leads to creative acts in celebration of freedom. Freedom also plays a predominant role in the lives of those convinced that "life's a beach," although this metaphor in support of self-indulgence is probably more of a reaction to the demands of contemporary living than a genuine life metaphor. There is no point in even trying to develop an exhaustive catalogue of life metaphors since humans have never tired of asking themselves and one another what it is to be human and how life should be lived, and people may embrace more than one life metaphor and shift between several in varying situations. Human aspirations, like life metaphors, always reach beyond conventional life.

The notion of life metaphors is useful because it suggests an organizing focus for moral vision, and moral vision is as important as derivational reasoning in understanding values and value differences among cultures as well as between individuals. Because moral vision is not reducible to proof-like argumentation, it tends to get expressed in nondiscursive forms. If we are asked for our reasons in support of a particular moral decision, we offer rules, moral criteria, our sense of the situation at hand, perhaps showing how our decision follows from these factors. And we can imagine getting into arguments with others who share our moral vision, about whether our decision is indeed derived correctly. But if we are asked for our reasons in support of our moral vision, we more likely offer images, refer to moral role models, talk about personal experiences including our sense of how we came to be who we are, and express our views with narrative accounts. We cannot articulate an argument in conventional terms that will compel others to accept our moral vision as their conclusion. Since nondiscursive expressions are often used in defense of moral visions, and since life metaphors are nondiscursive shorthand for the perspective from which we are oriented in our engagement of the world, asking for a description of someone's moral vision by way of a life metaphor can prompt them to convey their vision meaningfully where they may be at a loss if confined to conventional discourse. Of course, the point is not to pick a life metaphor from a list of options but for individuals each to articulate his or her own moral visions, to the extent it is helpful, by means of life metaphors.

Metaphors are common to ethical discourse in other ways as well. They bring depth and richness to literary explorations of morality for example. In a discussion of rationality in *Love's Knowledge*, Martha Nussbaum describes practical wisdom in Aristotelian terms, suggesting that decision procedures that consist of systems of rules still require people of good judgment to use them, at least when it comes to morality. For Nussbaum, such practical wisdom involves commitment "to rich descriptions of qualitative heterogeneity, context-sensitive perceiving, and to emotional and imaginative activity." Novels are particularly well suited to developing just this sensitivity of perception through expressing the complex, subtle, and detailed imagery necessary for a full understanding of context, without which good moral judgment is lost. This is the sort of practical wisdom that rationality requires, "not some simpler or neater thing."[8] No matter how precise the rules, they still must be interpreted and applied, and this is where the good judgment of practical wisdom comes in. Metaphoric imagery, unlike formal decision procedures, touches moral vision by drawing us into a way of seeing. In *Beloved*, Toni Morrison's deep and complex imagery draws readers into the world of nineteenth-century American slavery so effectively that we can comprehend an act too heinous for us to imagine before having read the novel. Morrison's narrative is so rich in creating Sethe's conviction, based on her own horrific experience, that we understand a mother believing she has to kill her child out of love, to save that child from slavery. The dense context of Sethe's world makes the simple application of a moral rule impossible. Entering the world of *Beloved* involves seeing things from a perspective different than the one we began with. Great novels change us, and often it is by challenging, deepening, and enlarging our moral vision beyond personal bias and conventional wisdom.

We can be drawn into a new way of seeing on a comprehensive scale, as is the case when our life metaphors are themselves altered, or on a scale covering a subset of our larger vision, perhaps effected by a lead metaphor addressing a specific area of life, or even a particular issue. For example, individuals functioning from within different life metaphors might agree that the suffering of animals should be reduced in our society and might organize around a lead metaphor that extends moral standing to animals by advocating animal rights. While talk of animal rights is common to us today, it is only recently that the metaphor stretching rights-talk to cover nonhuman animals has begun fading into general use. To enter and participate in the virtual world of the metaphoric expression is to envision things from a new and larger perspective, allowing us to form judgments from beyond the confines of conventional discourse and our personal biases.

Chinnagounder's Challenge is Deane Curtin's critique of environmental philosophy and exploration of the relationship between nature and human culture. For Curtin, values begin in local moral knowledge grounded in practices rather than in abstract rules or quantitative calculations. He distinguishes reiterative values, those that bind a culture together, from transformative values, which challenge the comfortable assumptions of the reiterative and stretch moral imagination. Since his context is globalization, his focus is on value contrasts, even collisions, encountered in travel to third-world places. Understanding in such a context involves the outsider internalizing enough of the local story to become a partial insider. Curtin tells us this involves a partial loss of self and is "not simply 'ethical' in the narrow sense of the term, but aesthetic."[9] Good moral judgment is aesthetic for Curtin as it is for Nussbaum because it requires imagination pulling us beyond conventionality, it carries us past routine and literal applications of rules, and whether the travel is actual or virtual, metaphor, imagery, any figurative expressions that draw us beyond ourselves are the elements of rationality that shape our moral visions and enlarge our practical wisdom.

Metaphors that animate the moral imagination sometimes provoke deep emotional engagement. Dostoevsky's underground man in *Notes from Underground*, a character obsessed with fear that industrialization would turn him into an organ stop, a lever, a cog in a gear of the machine of life, comes to mind, as does Ellison's *Invisible Man*, where whites get whiter by mixing in a few black servants, invisible as people but conspicuous as signs of status for the rich. The moral force is conveyed through the emotional suffering of characters and through readers identifying with those characters and emotions. While emotion is for the most part set aside in tradition ethical theory, emotion is central to moral struggle. For Nussbaum, "imagination and emotional response have a guiding role to play in perception and . . . are partly constitutive of moral knowledge."[10] Perhaps it is just this deep entanglement of imagination with emotion that makes metaphor an important link between emotion and reason. By giving figurative shape to ideas not yet expressible conventionally, metaphors provide connections otherwise unexpressed and thus unmade between thoughts and feelings. Rather than reinforcing the traditional contrast—even dichotomy—between reason and emotion, metaphor, by engaging imagination and emotion simultaneously, respects the integrated affective and cognitive aspects of thought. The aesthetic grasp is holistic, later to be analyzed and abstracted into constituent bits that then become difficult for theorists to reconnect.

It is just this holistic power of aesthetic expression that characterizes the dangers against which Plato warns in his *Republic*. Plato is notorious for having censored and banished artists from the city he has Socrates construct in order to defend the notion that we will live better lives if we choose justice over injustice. Plato had been an able poet himself as a young man, but allegedly turned from poetry to philosophy after Socrates' martyrdom. Those having read much Plato know that he never fully abandons poetry. His early and middle dialogues combine literary and philosophic achievement unparalleled since. How are we to understand his harsh treatment of poets and other artists in his *Republic*?

In Book One, Thrasymachus claims that "the life of an unjust person is better than that of a just one" and Socrates argues him into submission.[11] Book

Two opens with Glaucon insisting that Socrates only "charmed" Thrasy-machus "as if he were a snake," and he presses Socrates to explain justice and injustice and the "power each itself has when it's by itself in the soul," leaving out of account their implications, so any choice between them is not made based on expected rewards or punishments. Glaucon renews the argument by means of a metaphor. The ring of Gyges allows its wearer to become invisible by a turn of the ring, thus able to act with impunity. With this as his vehicle, Glaucon constructs a scenario where a perfectly just individual has a reputation for injustice, and a perfectly unjust individual has a reputation for justice, each receiving the rewards or punishments of reputation, not reality. So, why be just? Wouldn't a rational person rather *seem* to be just than be so? It is at this point that Plato has Socrates use a metaphor of his own: he suggests that it may be easier to see justice and injustice in something larger, so the discussion turns to the city, a metaphor for the individual. Cities arise because individuals are not self-sufficient, and justice turns out to be a balanced interdependence to meet needs for food, clothing, shelter, and personal relationships (the metaphor suggesting that just individuals enjoy a healthy balance of material, emotional, and intellectual needs, the aspects of their tri-part self being interdependent like the citizens of the city). While Socrates is satisfied with life in his simple, healthy city, Glaucon insists on a luxurious city; Socrates calls it "fevered," but is willing to discuss it since justice and injustice will be found there too. It is in the luxury city, the one "surrendered . . . to the endless acquisition of money"[12] that we find the outrages reminiscent of *Brave New World*: censorship, a professional military, euthanasia, eugenics, and a caste system supported by lies, along with control and banishment of poets, musicians, and artists. The self that corresponds to this city is equally unbalanced.

Traditionally read with little imagination and even less concern for the second half of the dialogue, in which education plays a prominent role in transforming the city, Plato and his *Republic* are often ridiculed for idealizing a closed society.[13] Setting aside the interpretation of Plato's political philosophy, one thing abundantly clear in *Republic* is that *if* the goal of a society is efficient accumulation of wealth, *then*, among other horrors, poets, musicians, and artists need to be controlled, because they can affect citizens powerfully and deeply, often provoking them to question or abandon their political leaders. Although it is rarely emphasized in discussions of Plato on the arts, artists are readmitted to the city late in *Republic*. In Book Ten, in the context of the ancient quarrel between poetry and philosophy, the charms of poetry are considered significant because of their potential influence. We are warned that taking poetry seriously can steer us from truth, can disrupt our efforts to be good, can tempt us away from attending to our integrity, and can lead us to neglecting justice and the rest of virtue.[14] Plato understands the seductive powers of the aesthetic.

The value of this digression into Plato comes from taking note of his insight into the powerful influence that the arts can have over our aspirations for living well. Aesthetic expressions can and do constitute important elements of our moral lives. But we are well served by Plato's warning, since aesthetic influence can mislead, tempt, and misdirect as well as guide and inspire our struggles for good lives. Plato readmits artists to the city only after both warning against these dangers and providing an antidote to their potentially harmful sway, namely, the critical reflections of philosophy helping us to keep our focus on truth and to guard against the seductive powers of the arts. As long as philosophy is available to keep the arts in check, artists are welcome in the city.

Certainly aesthetic expressions have amazing seductive power. Propaganda, whether to sell products or to manipulate and exploit political views, can be highly misleading and destructive in the absence of critical reasoning to check abuses. Metaphors can convey corrupt as well as constructive moral visions. Chattel slavery could persist in part because huge numbers of citizens saw the world through lenses that excluded black people from the ranks of humanity, and slavery was undone in part by exposing and destroying that lie. Warriors have justified their carnage in part by regarding the enemy as less than fully human, so we have a litany of dehumanizing epithets for enemies: redskins, japs, krauts, gooks, rag-heads, and so on, ad nauseam. Racists both enrage and inspire with racial slurs, sexists with gender put-downs, heterosexists with crude and hateful labels, and often the bigoted words are metaphoric and not literal, provoking images that entangle imagination, emotion, morality, and immorality. Such metaphors can be visual as well, with racist, sexist, and heterosexist images reinforcing negative stereotypes. Surely their aesthetic power adds to their destructiveness by grabbing, engaging, provoking, and holding our attention.

In the absence of critical reasoning to challenge abusive, destructive, and hateful expressions, such images can animate imaginations in powerful, lively, and seductive ways and encourage bigoted attitudes, beliefs, and acts. This is why careful, clear, and critical reasoning is needed for moral thought to be balanced and worthy of conviction. But the necessity of such sobering cognitive work does not make it sufficient for moral thought. As we have seen, aesthetic aspects are central to moral reasoning as well, contributing a holistic grasp that constitutes the moral vision through which we engage the world. Metaphors allow us expression beyond the confines of conventional discourse, stretch us beyond conventional morality and personal biases, respect connections between emotion and cognition, and animate imagination by provoking active engagement among those who would understand them. Moral metaphors open moral reflection to new ways of orienting our thinking, challenge us through images in dissonance with our values, and push us to defend, deepen, refine, and sometimes abandon explicit statements of what had been our moral convictions. The aesthetic aspects of moral thought engender moral growth while more conventional moral reasoning works toward clarity and precision. Both are necessary.

The critical reasoning needed to check powerful moral metaphors is characteristic of conventional critical thought in requiring internal consistency, seeking conceptual clarity, testing explicit and implicit assertions against experience, weighing pros and cons against already accepted principles, and doing all of this openly in an effort to minimize bias. At the same time, such checks and balances have to respect aesthetic expressions as not fully reducible to conventional discourse. This is especially difficult outside of one's own culture. Moral thought functions at the edge of moral conventionality, and, as our globe continues to shrink, the interactions and collisions among different conventional moralities will continue to grow. In this context, the pressing challenge to moral thought is in resolving—or at least managing— moral conflict and reconciling conflicting parties. Historically, moral conflicts have often resulted in domination and submission, with one outlook prevailing over others, thus creating winners and losers. Occasionally, an accommodation of tolerance allows coexistence of multiple views. Contemporary moral theory has some theorists searching for moral universals, others suggesting the futility of such a search, some settling for context-specific values, some adopting moral skepticism, some returning to their own traditions, and more. So it is that we must turn next to the challenges of pluralism.

NOTES

1. See Curtin, Deane, *Chinnagounder's Challenge* (Bloomington: Indiana University Press, 1999), 169, and Danto, Arthur, *The Transfiguration of the Commonplace* (Cambridge, MA: Harvard University Press, 1981), 171–77.

2. Langer, Susanne, *Philosophy in a New Key* (Cambridge, MA: Harvard University Press, 1942), 141–42.

3. Langer, *Philosophy in a New Key*, 141–42.

4. Kuhn, Thomas, *The Structure of Scientific Revolutions* (Chicago: The University of Chicago Press, 1962, 1970), 5.

5. For a close analysis of metaphoric functions within moral *theory*, see Johnson, Mark, *Moral Imagination: Implications of Cognitive Science for Ethics* (Chicago: The University of Chicago Press, 1993).

6. King, Martin Luther, Jr., *Why We Can't Wait* (New York: New American Library, 1963, 1964), 73–95.

7. Murdoch, Iris, "Vision and Choice in Morality," *Proceedings of the Aristotelian Society*, 1956, in *Christian Ethics and Contemporary Philosophy*, ed. Ian Ramsey (New York: Macmillan Co., 1966), 40.

8. Nussbaum, Martha C., *Love's Knowledge* (Oxford, UK: Oxford University Press, 1990), 85–89.

9. Curtin, *Chinnagounder's Challenge*, 168.

10. Nussbaum, *Love's Knowledge*, 91.

11. Plato, *Republic*, 347e.

12. Plato, *Republic*, 373e.

13. For example, Popper, K. R., *The Open Society and Its Enemies*, (London, UK: Routledge, 1945). For a fuller discussion of this, see Cady, Duane L., "Individual Fulfillment (not social engineering) in Plato's *Republic*," *Idealistic Studies* Vol. 13, No. 3 (September, 1983), 240–49.

14. Plato, *Republic*, 608b.

Chapter Six

Ethics and Pluralism

When I do not see plurality stressed in the very structure of a theory, I know that I will have to do lots of acrobatics—like a contortionist or tight-rope walker to have this theory speak to me without allowing the theory to distort me in my complexity.

—Maria Lugones

The world has always been diverse. The variety of cultures and peoples is so wide that we can scarcely take it in. In discussing experience in context above I noted the broad sweep of human development described by Jared Diamond in *Guns, Germs and Steel*, a virtually continuous pattern of conflict among rival groups across human history, each group projecting its own interests, each acting in defense of its own way of life, each threatened by competition over limited resources, with all of them locked in an ongoing struggle to survive and flourish, and with little or no regard for the effects their flourishing may have on the others. Concerning contemporary development, I called attention to Wolfgang Sachs's claim that while over 5,000 languages were spoken around the globe in 1992, expectations were that only 100 or so would survive another fifty years, and that with the demise of languages comes the end of cultures. It seems that the broad pattern continues. Western modernization spreads into a global monoculture characterized by technological progress having priority over justice and economic interests typically trumping traditional values. Along with expanding Western cultural hegemony and subsequent changes in traditional communications, transportation, and markets come increased cross-cultural contact, mixing, and collisions. While tolerance for the sake of profit can follow self-interest, celebration of and respect for difference are nonmarket values and as such are themselves anachronistic to the global market. Ethics, searching for a right way of life, is increasingly seen as a quaint and lingering historical artifact, as a last refuge of tradition-alists, while sophisticated thinkers embrace a cosmopolitan relativism or even moral skepticism. Ethics gives way to economy and political realism.

We have seen these same patterns reflected historically in normative ethics, not only concerning the broad sweep of human cultures but also re-garding interpersonal morality within a single tradition. When individuals have conflicting moral claims, each attempts to bring the other to their way of seeing the issue, by subsuming the other's way of thinking under their own, convincing them of the advantages of one view over the other in the case at hand, converting them to one's own view, or simply imposing it on the other, if they have the means to do so. Putting it bluntly, traditional moral disagreement often reflects dogmatic absolutism: "I'm right; if we disagree, you're wrong." In this way, interpersonal value conflicts look a lot like the large-scale value conflicts arising across cultures. Of course, the more so-phisticated way of addressing moral conflict involves recognizing the legit-imacy of differing outlooks and conceding the reasonableness of alternative perspectives. Liberal nations do this with various legal protections guarding their citizens from having moral views imposed on them and protecting their rights to their own moral convictions, within bounds set by the state. Persis-tent conflicts get adjudicated in the courts. To be blunt again, this comes to "I'm right; if we disagree, maybe everyone is right in their own way." Ethi-cal theory has been struggling to avoid both of these options, absolutism and relativism. The first seems too insistent, confident to the point of arrogance. We admire people for acting on their convictions and for sticking to them, but we are mere mortals and we are not infallible. It may not be the case that there is one and only one correct set of values to guide us to a good life. The other option seems problematic as well, too tolerant, making morality vacu-ous by allowing any and all views equal standing. Prevailing standards are increasingly challenged as arbitrary, and there are no clear bases for resolv-ing moral conflict.

The situation at both levels has only gotten more difficult in recent decades as the globe continues to shrink due to mass communication and transporta-tion, compounded by millions of immigrants, many of them refugees, crossing traditional cultural boundaries and settling in contexts so different from those of their upbringing that decades of "progress" are traversed instantly. Individ-uals and groups with very different moral traditions are interacting with one another more than ever before, resulting in significant increase in cross-cultural understanding but also in significant value collisions. Both assimila-tion and segregation are common, depending in part on how easily and eagerly members of subordinate groups accept dominant values. For several hundred years, confidence in scientific reason inspired by seventeenth-, eighteenth-, and nineteenth-century European thinkers guided policies and practices as Western hegemony grew. Colonialism and neocolonialism reinforced a dominant Enlightenment outlook that is prevalent today. "Underdeveloped" places and people are expected to become increasingly like the self-proclaimed "developed" places and people. This is progress. (It rarely occurs to anyone to think of Europe and North America as overdeveloped, despite the immense human and environmental cost of their ways of life and the impossibility of such practices being adopted globally.)

The increase in interaction among dominant and subordinate groups has led to more and more criticism of prevailing institutions and individuals. Modernity is on the defensive on two major fronts. One criticism alleges hypocrisy, since the universal and unalienable rights seem to be held by and protected for only a small percentage of human beings, and, perhaps worse, that the few enjoying such rights do so at the expense of others. That is, the universals are not universal enough. A second major criticism suggests that they are too universal, that they insufficiently reflect the diversity of peoples and cultures and subsequently become part of cultural domination. "[W]hat is increasingly perceived as the crisis of modernity and modern values" can be understood by "drawing out the particularity that lurks beneath the universalist claims of the Enlightenment project which was, in theory, valid for humanity as a whole even if humanity was to be rather restrictively defined."[1]

Theorizing itself has a universalizing character but, as Maria Lugones reminds us, "the logic of all theorizing is affected by a recognition of difference."[2] During the second half of the twentieth century, theorists were pushed by events to develop expanding critiques of the Western intellectual tradition in order to expose persistent false universalizations, where particular notions get projected as if they are universals. The thinking involved in social changes, including women's suffrage, women entering the paid work force in large numbers, and civil rights campaigns to dismantle racial segregation, outstripped that of ethical theory. In an effort to bring theory up to speed with events, philosophers have had to acknowledge that many of the historic philosophic claims about human nature say more about the points of view of the theorists making the claims than they say about all human beings, since the perspectives and experiences of women, people of color, those from outside the theoried class, those embracing nondominant political, moral, or religious views had all been left out, largely because the theorists themselves were typically white men from the dominant segments of dominant cultures. Their ideas reflect their experience, and, as Nancy Holland puts it, "are offered as examples of human behavior," functioning "as standards that exclude those with different experiences from the realm of the human."[3] Those falsely universalizing from particular experience to standards for humanity are often advantaged by "the power hidden in universalization, the power to say who and what other people are, and the power to ignore their self-definitions and their own experience of themselves and the world."[4] But difference is not genuinely recognized with a mere disclaimer admitting the inevitable limits of perspective. Genuine recognition of difference requires understanding it interactively. For Lugones, this means acknowledging not only that our perspective has left out others but that those other perspectives are like mirrors held up to us: they reflect truths about us that we do not otherwise see and that we may not want to accept.

The case of race is of particular interest here. Highlighting selective perception, Lugones quotes Marilyn Frye's observation that "whitely people have a staggering faith in their own rightness and goodness, and that of other whitely people."[5] Such folks block identification with the images in the mirrors of the perspectives of others who are different in order to preserve the self-image of their own perspective that is reflected in those like themselves who surround them. The modern, enlightenment notion of progress with its sense of civilization improving steadily through the guidance of impartial, scientific rationality provides insulation from the reflections in those mirrors of the different others. This is why it is important to be reminded that "scientific racism [is] one of modernity's more durable intellectual products,"[6] despite the fact that people of color are nearly invisible in modernity's accounts of itself. When we think of modernity, we think of science and technology, progress, enlightenment, liberalism, democracy, capitalism, individualism, and perhaps less often, of imperialism. Rarely are slavery and racism listed as central features of modernity. As Gilroy tells us, "Eurocentric rationalism . . . banishes the slave experience from its accounts of modernity" even though "racial terror is not merely compatible with occidental rationality but cheerfully complicit with it."[7] Although even ancient texts acknowledge differences in skin color among people, the concept of race is not ancient; it is a modern scientific notion but one that does not conform to the current standards of science.

K. Anthony Appiah documents both a history of the modern scientific concept of race and the contemporary evidence, also scientific, for denying meaningfulness to the concept. He notes that "not only is race . . . a concept that is invoked to explain cultural and social phenomena, it is also grounded in the physical and the psychological natures of different races; it is, in other words, what we would call a biological concept."[8] This leads us to *racialism*, Appiah's term for the belief that "there are heritable characteristics, possessed by members of our species, which allow us to divide them into a small set of races, in such a way that all the members of these races share certain traits and tendencies with each other that they do not share with members of any other race."[9] The concept gains increasing currency in the nineteenth century, even appearing in the full title of Charles Darwin's landmark work, *The Origin of Species by Means of Natural Selection or the Preservation of Favored Races in the Struggle for Life*.[10] With science taking the biological concept of race seriously, ordinary use of the term was, in a sense, underwritten by the expertise of science that was gaining in stature as the paradigm of knowledge. But a contemporary genetic understanding exposes racialism as, simply, mistaken. As it turns out, "in humans, however you define the major races, the biological variability within them is almost as great as the biological variation within the species as a whole."[11] What this means is that race is a social construction, a label that clusters a handful of physical characteristics like skin color and hair type but carries no other characteristics along. As Appiah puts it, "the truth is that there are no races."[12] The labels are no more meaningful than would be calling left-handed blue-eyed people a certain race. One can imagine a social context in which such labels have meaning, but all they would do is cluster people by the defining characteristics; they have no scientific significance whatsoever.

We might wonder why a culture would be eager for science to legitimize racialism. Perhaps it had to do to some extent with a nagging awareness of the moral horrors of slavery. One way to rationalize the obscenity of owning and exploiting people; of treating them worse than domestic animals were treated; and of destroying their lives, their families, and their cultures would be to mistake an ideology for a fact of nature, to believe that somehow biology reinforced the status that society conveyed. If blacks were scientifically known to be inferior to whites, it would bring some authoritative sense to the otherwise incomprehensible and outrageous mistreatment of blacks, and it would ease the dissonance between lived experience and the egalitarian principles of the nation's founding documents. If so prestigious an institution as science could offer its blessing to racialism, then the heinous institution of racism could stand, and with it the economic benefits of uncompensated labor and the social privileges of white supremacy. People in dominant groups could repress any thought that their status was unfairly gained, could feel good about themselves and their skin-color advantages, could feel as though the advantages were natural and thus warranted. If science affirmed race, the alleged hypocrisy of modernity would be defeated. But, as Appiah demonstrates, science does not confirm racialism, at least not any more. The problem is that it did for at least two centuries and that social customs have reinforced a racial hierarchy.

Now we find ourselves in a world where race is a mistaken belief but where racism is a fact of life. There are no racial essences, yet discrimination and unfairness based on skin color are quite real. In response to racism, people band together both to support one another and to oppose racial injustice. People have racial identities, partly based on attributes ascribed to them by others, partly based on attributes they identify with and choose, and find themselves at various levels in our racially stratified culture, usually the lighter their skin tone the higher their status on the color scale. The dilemma is that racial identities reify—make real—the concept of race that itself has no basis in nature. Exposing the fiction of race does not automatically dismantle hundreds of years of social practices that reinforce racism. So science has been a disappointing model for reasoning about race at least twice: first, in giving its authority to the mistake, thus helping racialized thinking to become more deeply entrenched in our culture, and second, in not being powerful enough to rid us of racism as it dispels the notion of race.

There are several lessons here, none of them new but all worth repeating. One is that scientific knowledge is fallible, not absolute, and that it changes over time. Another is that science is not impartial, apolitical, amoral, and objective; these may be aspirations of most scientists, but science itself is practiced by human beings who each have their own values, perspectives, and limitations. Still another lesson is that scientific reasoning is not as different from other forms of reasoning as stereotypes suggest; like practical reasoning as well as aesthetic, moral, economic, and so on, science has limits, requires integrity of its practitioners, and stands to benefit from regular criticism from other forms of reason. Perhaps this is the most important lesson. Rather than putting science on a pedestal and modeling other forms of reason after it, perhaps we should recognize the strengths and limitations of scientific thought— and the strengths and limitations of other forms of reason—as well as recognize the aspects of various forms of thought as they mix and interact.

In *The Politics of Reality*, Marilyn Frye underscores the significance and power of social constructions that are taken to be features of nature. "For efficient subordination, what's wanted is that the structure not appear to be a cultural artifact kept in place by human decision or custom, but that it appear *natural*."[13] "To be white is to be a member of an in-group, a kin group, which is self-defining."[14] While our skin pigmentation is natural, group affiliation is social. Society classifies us into groups by virtue of our skin color, and a host of advantages go automatically to members of dominant groups while disadvantages go to members of subordinate groups. None of us created this system, the cultural institutions and practices through which advantages and disadvantages are implemented, but we know the consequences are inevitable, unearned, and unfair. We cannot change our pigmentation, but we can resist unfair structures and renounce affiliation with such groups. As Frye puts it, "white supremacy is *not* a law of nature, nor is any individual's complicity in it."[15]

Gender hierarchies also rely on social constructions functioning as if they are natural.

> If one thinks there are biologically deep differences between women and men which cause and justify divisions of labor and responsibility such as we see in the modern patriarchal family and male-dominated workplace, one may *not* have arrived at this belief because of direct experience of unmolested physical evidence, but because our customs serve to construct that appearance.[16]

All of us grow up under enormous social pressure to act feminine or masculine, to dress the part, adopt appropriate speech patterns, mannerisms, body language, to "fix" our physical shortcomings by cosmetics, diet, exercise, hormone therapy, surgery, and so on, all to reinforce the cultural demand for "a world where men are men and women are women and there is nothing in between and nothing ambiguous."[17] No doubt a good many folks take this obsessive genderizing to be natural rather than merely customary, and one result is that most accept traditional gender roles. A kind of gender hegemony emerges, and one way of being overwhelms other options by regarding the others as unnatural, perverse, deviant, or abnormal.

The situation is even more difficult for those who do not adhere to social constraints regarding whom it may be thought appropriate for them to love. As Marilyn Frye puts it, "In a culture in which one is deemed sinful, sick or disgusting (at least) if one is not heterosexual, it is very important to keep track of one's sexual feelings and the sexes of those who inspire them."[18] No wonder the obsession around announcing one's sex through clothing, manner, hairstyle, and body language.

> Heterosexual critics of queers' "role-playing" ought to look at themselves in the mirror on their way out for a night on the town to see who's in drag. The answer is, everybody is. Perhaps the main difference between heterosexuals and queers is that when queers go forth in drag, they know they are engaged in theater — they are playing and they know they are playing. Heterosexuals usually are taking it all perfectly seriously, thinking they are in the real world, thinking they *are* the real world.[19]

This is an important insight. Members of dominant groups take their socially constructed world to be natural in part because the world really is *their* world, it works to their advantage. Members of subordinate groups do not have this luxury. Just as DuBois notes the necessity of blacks seeing themselves not only as they appear to themselves but also as they are seen by dominant society, Frye notes the necessity of gays and lesbians seeing themselves as they are seen; in both cases, well-being, even survival, may depend on it.

The irony is that members of subordinated groups have a better understanding of what is going on because they must; members of dominant groups can remain comfortably oblivious, not even noticing the social structures that provide them with advantages, imagining that merit alone accounts for their well-being, secured in self-deceptive conceptual frameworks or self-deluding moral visions. Although often ignored, sometimes even invisible, members of subordinate groups dare not be oblivious; for them, knowing dominant as well as subordinate culture is a condition of life. For Frye, as for Lugones, the mirrors are important. They make it possible for dominant group members to gain more complete and more accurate pictures of themselves. This is why pluralism is important. If we want to know what's really going on, we need to check our pictures of reality against something other than dominant social constructions. All of us need mirrors—the mirrors of those others, different from ourselves, who see the world from perspectives very unlike ours.

The necessity of a pluralistic check on our self-images gains importance with our relative power, since the more powerful we are the more we are likely to be surrounded with people trying to please us out of respect for or deference to our power. This functions between individuals, among groups, at various levels of scale. When we shift from the diversity of people and perspectives within a single nation, dominated by its historic traditions, to consider international manifestations of cultural difference, the problem of power is magnified. Western global hegemony grows not only due to expanding Western economic, political, and military interests, but also because of the deference paid to wealthy and powerful nations, corporations, and individuals by poor and weak nations, organizations, and individuals, out of a complex mix of fear, envy, resentment, awe, hope, jealousy, and self-interest. Just as on the smaller scale, those in dominant positions internationally need the insights and perspectives of others if they are genuinely to know what's going on. They need to look carefully and seriously into the mirrors held up to them by those different others in order to check their self-image against something outside their own partial judgment and thus gain a more complete understanding.

Pluralism becomes crucial as an alternative to both the insistence on one and only one objective system of values leading to the good life on the one hand, and the acceptance of any and all values as mere subjective preferences on the other. While it is true that traditional claims to a single absolute and universal value system valid for humans everywhere at all times have given way to increasingly relativistic notions of values, the shift may be due to the plurality of meaningful values rather than to an erosion of absolutes leading to collapse into relativism as suggested by the absolutist/relativist dichotomy.[20] Or it may be due to the wide variety of perspectives, each focusing on aspects of the good life that are especially pressing in their particular cultural and historic contexts. What we need is a way to understand values as meaningful yet at the same time neither arbitrary nor necessarily absolute.

Maria Lugones builds on Marilyn Frye's notion of arrogant perception, the practice of seeing with arrogant eyes that organize everything around the interests of the perceiver,[21] noting that women are not only objects of men's arrogant perception but can themselves be arrogant perceivers, as all of us can, based on class or color or other differences. Lugones suggests the possibility of "world-traveling," entering alternative contexts and their visions of reality, moving from one's usual conceptual framework to another, shifting from participation as an insider in one realm to become something of an insider in another. One can inhabit a "world" in which one is an academic, for example, or one can leave it to enter the world of one's extended family, none who are, or even fully grasp what it is to be, academics. Worlds can be large—being an American, for example—or quite small and even idiosyncratic, a peculiar subset of a larger world, like that of a Korean American adoptee raised as an atheist on a goat farm in rural North Dakota. We may understand the way in which a given world constructs us and the way we construct it, or not, and we may or may not identify with it. If we are at ease in any particular world, then we are fluent in it; we know the norms of behavior and are confident. Or we are at ease because we accept the norms. Or we are at ease because we are with those we love and they love us. Or because we have a shared history. We may or may not be at some degree of ease in any of the various worlds we inhabit. Some are entered at great risk, entered of necessity, and inhabited with caution; others are entered lovingly, in which case entering another's world can be "a way of identifying with them . . . because by traveling to their 'world' we can understand *what it is to be them and what it is to be ourselves in their eyes*,"[22] if not completely, then at least partially.

Appiah warns us that "collective identities have a tendency . . . to 'go imperial.'"[23] Lugones warns of something similar when she sees the "imperial eye" as an international/intercultural variation of the "arrogant eye."[24] Both recognize with Frye that an antidote to arrogant perception is taking seriously the images in the mirrors held up to us by the different others with whom we interact, especially the others subordinated by dominant outlooks and institutions, to begin practicing at least humble if not loving perception. We reduce the risk of arrogant perception to the extent that we are genuinely and personally interactive as we guard against reading our own experience and perspective as if they are universal. World traveling helps, especially as we risk entering worlds critical of our own, worlds where we are likely to be uncomfortable. This can involve big steps, for example living with locals for weeks or months in a cultural setting radically different from our own, or a much smaller but nevertheless threatening step, like reading a radical critique of our own ethics or politics, or taking a philosophy class. Genuine openness to a plurality of values and perspectives helps us, if only to remind ourselves that we have no monopoly on truth, individually or culturally. Deane Curtin suggests that one must become at least a partial insider to a practice to claim authority. This means integrating theoretical and practical wisdom, respecting the day-to-day working knowledge of ordinary people sufficiently to gain hands-on experience for oneself, and not imposing expert scientific knowledge from outside and above a context; that is, it means countering arrogant with humble perception, with open willingness to enter, participate in, and be changed by another world.

Recognizing a plurality, a multiplicity of worlds and, subsequently, of values, is an important step away from the dogmatic absolutism that often characterizes cultural and ethical conflict. It is easy to understand why taking this step seems threatening to many, and why it is often interpreted as abandoning universal values for relativism. But one need not embrace value relativism by acknowledging pluralism. Recognizing the legitimacy of different sets of context-bound values, which are neither arbitrary nor mere preferences yet which are limited in their range of applicability to the cultural contexts in which they arise, is acknowledging that meaning varies with context. While very different from those of another context, such bounded values, by having their meaning only within their contexts and thus by not being read as universal, do not threaten other value contexts in the way that dogmatic absolute values do. They do not "go imperial" because the recognition of pluralism keeps them context bound. "Three strikes and you're out" is meaningful in the context of a baseball game, but not meaningful in a chess match. This does not make it arbitrary or a mere preference, since it is related to other aspects of the nature of baseball; rather, it recognizes its meaning as bound to its context. In a similar way, showing respect within a hierarchical system involves paying deference to those above and leads one to expect deference from those below; chain of command structures depend on such a context for their effectiveness. But there are other ways of showing respect in other contexts. In egalitarian structures, respect is horizontal rather than vertical, and it could be insulting to defer to or to expect deference from a sister or brother, partner, coworker, or colleague. Recognizing different forms of respect in different contexts need not generate allegedly absolute and universal claims about respect, nor need it lead to insistence that the notion is arbitrary, nor must it result in a ranking of superior and inferior forms of respect. There are simply different forms in different contexts.

Of course, values arising in one context may "travel" to another without necessarily going imperial. While values arise in cultural contexts, they need not be completely limited in their range of applicability to the context in which they arise, so they may be appropriated to other contexts. If the notion of human rights arose in a European context, this needn't limit its significance to Europe any more than a scientific discovery in one context need be limited in its applications to its context of origin. Notions "go imperial" when they are imposed by constraint from the outside. But ideas that serve well in one culture may be taken in and prove useful in another if enough of those in the new context identify with them and choose them. Values, like technologies, may spread by imposition, theft, adaptation, and other variations. Whereas dogmatism insists on one way and relativism accepts all and any ways, pluralism opens doors to give and take, adaptation, and customization.

Another advantage to pluralism is its emphasis on the limitations of any single perspective, underscoring human fallibility and pointing to the importance of collaborative and collective wisdom, not only within a single culture, but at cross-cultural and international levels as well. Gandhi's moral vision is oriented around devotion to truth. *Satyagraha*, literally "holding on to truth" or "truth force" is his central notion. For Gandhi, nonviolence follows directly: devotion to truth excludes the use of violence because human beings are "not capable of knowing the absolute truth and, therefore, not competent to punish."[25] One cannot overemphasize Gandhi's devotion to truth, which he says is "the sole justification for our existence," insisting that "it is more correct to say that Truth is God than to say God is Truth."[26] Gandhi recognizes the dangers of dogmatic devotion to truth, suggesting that "what may appear as truth to one person will often appear as untruth to another person." But he dispels the threat of dogmatism, assuring us that "where there is honest effort it will be realized that what appear to be different truths are like the countless and different leaves of the same tree."[27] Whether one reads this image as suggesting multiple aspects of one truth or multiple partial truths all contributing to a more complete vision, clearly pluralism is his point. Arrogant perception goes hand-in-hand with dogmatism; presuming to know absolutely and universally entails imposing such knowledge on others. Skeptical perception goes hand-in-hand with relativism; denying the possibility of genuine knowledge entails accepting any and all values as equals. Humble or loving perception avoids both absolutism and relativism. It goes hand in hand with pluralism, respecting diverse meanings in diverse contexts, and cherishing the variety of perspectives because each partial view contributes to a more complete understanding. None of this is to say that universal or absolute values are impossible; rather, it says that limitations on human knowledge make dogmatic claims to universal, absolute values untenable. We may continue aspiring to such values, and make provisional claims proposing candidates for universal and absolute status, but pluralism asks us to remain open to a more complete view that may result from considering the perspectives of diverse others.

Pluralism is a hard sell. Sometimes it is rejected because it is confused with relativism, sometimes because it is threatening to absolute claims. Perhaps the greatest obstacle to a widespread embrace of pluralism is that all of us tend to be attached to our own perspectives and values, typically those of the contexts we know best, the ones in which we have been nurtured, and people of prominence often appeal to and even exploit those attachments. The vast majority of human beings are vulnerable to having their fears of others enlarged by such exploitation because most humans have very limited opportunities for nonthreatening interactions with very different others. For most people, existing cultural and international structures and institutions impose conditions that virtually eliminate chances for nonthreatening interaction across the various boundaries and barriers, of race, class, gender, religion, language, and more. This leaves us in a given reality that has been socially constructed but that nonetheless limits what is possible in the way of dramatic change. As we have seen, the fact that race is a mistaken belief does not eliminate the social reality of racism; recognizing the social construction of gender hierarchies across most cultures does not eliminate unfair and unequal conditions for women globally; understanding how a few nations have taken advantage of the geophysical head-starts provided to them by chance does not eliminate exploitation under the name of global development. So, reconceiving values as genuinely pluralistic rather than either absolute or relative does not, by itself, stop or undo the many wrongs against disadvantaged others carried out by advantaged individuals and nations. As I have emphasized above, these problems are not merely intellectual problems, and they cannot be resolved by theory alone. The "world-traveling" needed involves nondiscursive, experiential, and aesthetic aspects as well as scientific and theoretical. The next step, the step beyond accepting and internalizing pluralism, is doing the hard work of changing institutions and practices to reflect and respect difference.

A good beginning is to shift value conflicts away from a focus on determining who is right and who is wrong toward a focus on creative and constructive negotiations that allow those holding competing values and value systems to resolve conflicts without having to sacrifice their most deeply held beliefs. Not every conflict gets the win-win outcome that is sought, but aspiring to it persistently, rather than aspiring to defeat other values and prevail with one's own, does alter the nature of conflict and the prospects for resolution. One key to any pluralistic effort is to minimize the extent to which conflicts are resolved by mere assertions of power, for such patterns lead to allegations that the dominating values are merely arbitrary. Genuine pluralism involves respect for the variety of perspectives as well as efforts at mutual understanding, and includes give and take among conflicting parties. The trust required is built through internalizing practices, sometimes by structuring procedures, which reduce assertions of narrow self-interest and look to the whole, often by involving disinterested third parties in arbitration and reconciliation of conflicts. Will this work every time? No, but moving the focus past either competing absolutes or competing arbitrary preferences to a pluralist effort at resolving conflicts with minimal loss and maximal gain to contesting parties changes the nature of conflict by opening the possibility of a positive outcome for everyone involved. Imagining it possible can set the stage for the actual.

What about human rights? Are they not absolute and universal? What about claims that no human being should have to endure torture or arbitrary arrest, that no one should be denied rights to assemble peaceably, to free speech, to participate in her or his governance, to enjoy freedom to worship as one chooses or not worship at all, and to expect fair and equal treatment before the law? None of what is said here denies the legitimacy of these and other such claims as candidates for universal values. The point here is that we are mere mortals, fallible and self-interested, with limited perspectives, and thus that our best claims to universality should be seen as provisional, tentative assertions of our best collective thinking, always in need of critique and refinement. As Jacob Bronowski pointed out years ago along with many others before him going back at least as far as Socrates, the most dangerous people who do the most harm are those who claim to have the absolute and universal corner on truth. At the concentration camp and crematorium at Auschwitz, standing in the shallows of a pond into which the ashes of four million people were flushed, Bronowski, reaching into the silt, reminds us that this outrageous mass murder "was not done by gas. It was done by arrogance. It was done by dogma. It was done by ignorance. When people believe they have absolute knowledge . . . this is how they behave."[28] Hiroshima or Nagasaki might be examples as well, or slavery, or ethnic cleansing, or various genocidal efforts. In aspiring to be gods, we can make ourselves worse than beasts.

To many, this aspiration to pluralism will sound absurdly naive and optimistic. But, then, to many a 100 years ago, the thought of a pacifist revolution forcing the British colonial power to allow India political independence was absurdly naive and optimistic. To many fifty years ago, the last thing expected was an articulate black minister leading a nonviolent movement to deconstruct then lawful racial segregation in America. To many fifteen years ago, the thought that Nelson Mandela could spend twenty-seven years in prison as a banned person under apartheid, yet negotiate the terms of his own release from within his prison cell and be elected president in a South Africa committed to nonracial politics and government was past naive to ridiculous; fifteen years ago, everyone knew that dismantling apartheid would involve a bloodbath. This is precisely why we need to rethink moral reasoning, because "impossible," "unthinkable," "irrational" events and individuals move morality in constructive and unexpected ways, through their actions, their expressions, and their visions, leaving formal, academic ethical theory lagging behind. Parallel to shifting paradigms in science, if we are to understand forms of reason in ethics, we need to open ourselves to a wider range of sources, a richer notion of reason, and a more robust role for moral imagination. Taking pluralism seriously is an alternative to being stuck in the absolutist/relativist dichotomy and allows us to imagine that what is taken to be impossible may not be so.

NOTES

1. Gilroy, Paul, *The Black Atlantic* (Cambridge, MA: Harvard University Press, 1993), 43.

2. Lugones, Maria, "On the Logic of Pluralist Feminism," in *Feminist Ethics*, ed. Claudia Card (Lawrence: University Press of Kansas, 1991), 37.

3. Holland, Nancy, *Is Women's Philosophy Possible?* (Lanham, MD: Rowman & Littlefield, 1990), 12.

4. Holland, *Is Women's Philosophy Possible?*, 2.

5. Lugones, "On the Logic of Pluralist Feminism," 42.

6. Gilroy, *The Black Atlantic*, 44.

7. Gilroy, *The Black Atlantic*, 54, 56.

8. Appiah, K. Anthony, "Race, Culture, Identity: Misunderstood Connections," in *Color Conscious: The Political Morality of Race*, with Amy Gutmann (Princeton, NJ: Princeton University Press, 1996), 49.

9. Appiah, K. Anthony, *In My Father's House: Africa in the Philosophy of Culture* (Oxford, UK: Oxford University Press, 1992), 13.

10. Appiah, "Race, Culture, Identity," 64.

11. Appiah, "Race, Culture, Identity," 68.

12. Appiah, *In My Father's House*, 45.

13. Frye, Marilyn, *The Politics of Reality* (Trumansburg, NY: The Crossing Press, 1983), 34, emphasis in the original.

14. Frye, *The Politics of Reality*, 115.

15. Frye, *The Politics of Reality*, 126.

16. Frye, *The Politics of Reality*, 35.

17. Frye, *The Politics of Reality*, 25.

18. Frye, *The Politics of Reality*, 22.

19. Frye, *The Politics of Reality*, 29.

20. Kekes, John, *The Morality of Pluralism* (Princeton, NJ: Princeton University Press, 1993), 15.

21. Frye, *The Politics of Reality*, 67.

22. Lugones, Maria, "Playfulness, 'World'-Traveling and Loving Perception," *Hypatia* 2, 2 (Summer, 1987), pp. 3–19, in *Women, Knowledge and Reality*, eds. Ann Garry and Marilyn Pearsall (Boston, MA: Unwin Hyman), 289.

23. Appiah, "Race, Culture, Identity," 103.

24. Lugones, "On the Logic of Pluralist Feminism," 39.

25. Gandhi, Mohandas K., *Non-Violent Resistance*, ed. Bharatan Kumarappa (New York: Schocken Books, 1951, 1961), 3.

26. Gandhi, *Non-Violent Resistance*, 38.

27. Gandhi, *Non-Violent Resistance*, 39.

28. Bronowski, Jacob, *The Ascent of Man* (Boston: Little, Brown and Company, 1973), 374.

Chapter Seven

Moral Thinking

None of us knows the steps and there's no music playing. And it doesn't stop with us. The whole world is doing it all the time. Open a newspaper and what do you read? America has bumped into Russia, England is bumping into India, rich man bumps into poor man. Those are big collisions. . . . They make for a lot of bruises. People get hurt in all that bumping, and we're sick and tired of it now. It's been going on for too long. Are we never going to get it right? Learn to dance life like champions instead of always being just a bunch of beginners at it?

—Athol Fugard

Normal moral thought takes place routinely while living life oriented by values that are so deeply internalized that acting on them is second nature to us. Decisions and choices are made out of deference to the internalized values. They may be values of the tradition in which we grew up, or values of another tradition we came to embrace, or a mix of values we have settled on. The point is that the values themselves are not up for grabs in normal moral thought; they have been accepted, and the thinking that goes on is to determine their application to the situations that life presents. Sometimes we derive our decision from basic principles of our values, but more often we interpret the situation by habit to fall under a rule laid down by our tradition, a rule, explicit or implicit, which expresses our values as it gets applied, our way of reading the situation reflecting how tightly or loosely we have come to live our values in our practices.

Things happen to us that provoke us to call our own values into question. We might find ourselves in situations where we know what our values call us to do, but we feel significant dissonance between the moral demands on us and the actions we are willing to undertake. For example, in Birmingham in 1963 during demonstrations to integrate lunch counters in downtown department stores, firefighters were deployed to clear demonstrators by training high-pressure fire hoses on them. At one turning point, Bull Connor, commissioner of public safety, ordered the hoses turned on to break up a prayer meeting of demonstrators.

> What happened in the next thirty seconds was one of the most fantastic events of the Birmingham story. Bull Connor's men, their deadly hoses poised for action, stood facing the marchers. The marchers, many of them on their knees, stared back, unafraid and unmoving. Slowly the Negroes stood up and began to advance.
>
> Connor's men, as though hypnotized, fell back, their hoses sagging uselessly in their hands while several hundred Negroes marched past them, without further interference, and held their prayer meeting as planned.[1]

The firefighters knew their duty was to follow Connor's orders, yet they couldn't any longer bring themselves to assault peaceful demonstrators. The dissonance they felt between their duty and the situation led them to override duty. Episodes of dissonance sometimes result in crisis, where our actions break with our values. If we later feel sufficiently guilty, we might resolve to stick to our values next time; if not, we might find ourselves rationalizing an exception for the case in question, or we might even break from the values we had held, either for different or for revised values.

Crises differ in magnitude and frequency. Members of relatively isolated communities are unlikely to undergo frequent, major moral crises because of the homogeneity of their practices and beliefs. Those from communities living in close proximity with diverse others have regular contact with different ways of life and subsequently have to accommodate the moral dissonance they experience, by resolutely holding on to their own way of life, or by compromising on some things, or by assimilating alternative values. When relatively isolated communities are forced into contact and interaction with outsiders, their ways of life are threatened and cultural crises are immanent, especially if there are significant power differences between the disparate communities, or if some are subordinated to others. Intercultural contact, both by choice and imposed from outside against the wishes of many traditionalists, continues to grow due to increased use of transportation and mass communication, and to the ever-widening economic globalization led by Western Europe and North America. Cultural clashes, and with them value collisions, are on the rise. Traditional ways of coping with the resulting tensions have, for the most part, been dogmatic, with dominant institutions expecting accommodation from subordinate groups, and with subordinate groups resisting to varying degrees. The traditional alternative to dogmatism has been a minority relativist plea for toleration.

While normal ethical thought continues apace, ethical theory consolidates, refines, articulates, and makes more precise the general principles and rule structures of various ethical frameworks, making adjustments along the way to accommodate minor internal inconsistencies and to embrace new situations as they arise. And so it is that Kantian deontologists and Millian consequentialists perform continuing maintenance on the dominant ethical frameworks, offering subtle and sometimes ingenious refinements to handle challenges from other Kant and Mill scholars. Some critics of ethical theory—for example, Alasdair MacIntyre and Richard Rorty discussed in chapter one above—raise difficulties of such breadth and depth that they call into question the whole enterprise of maintaining Kantian and utilitarian ethical theory, suggesting a return to foundational beliefs now lost or claiming that philosophy cannot do what it has set out to do.

In the meantime, feminism has responded to crisis—traditional philosophy having been practiced almost exclusively by men and thus not having reflected the experience and perspectives of women—by articulating feminist ethical theory. While some defenders of Kant and Mill see no crisis and others reinterpret texts in an effort to make them appropriately inclusive, feminist ethics has nonetheless gained a secure foothold in professional circles.

This same pattern is playing itself out regarding another apparent crisis for ethical theory, the traditional absence of theorists of color and thus of experiences and perspectives of people of color. Perhaps because there are relatively few people of color practicing in professional circles of ethical theory, or perhaps due to defensiveness among traditional theorists on issues of color, or due to some combination of these and other factors, this area of study has not yet found wide acceptance in textbook ethics. To appropriate an observation from Thomas Kuhn, we can say that in ethics, as he observes regarding natural science, "novelty emerges only with difficulty, manifested by resistance, against a background provided by expectation."[2]

For Kuhn, crisis provokes destructive and constructive paradigm changes. In science, technical breakdown is the core of crisis, when dominant theoretical frameworks are confronted with experiential data that cannot be accounted for, thus prompting novel theory as a response. In ethics, the standards for failure and breakdown are less clear and less widely accepted; perhaps MacIntyre or Rorty have identified breakdown, but it may be generations before such signals would be widely recognized as having come. This is partly because it is difficult to interpret history while it is happening, but mostly because ethical systems involve radically different notions of success or failure than do scientific theories. As we have seen above, ethical thought is considerably more complicated than that of science, at least insofar as it achieves far less clarity over what constitutes evidence in support of claims, enjoys far less deference to experts or authorities in the field, achieves less in the way of general agreement around what counts as success or failure, and faces a more diverse array of theoretical options at any given moment. Science has achieved a kind of hegemonic authority status that is reinforced by conventional methods broadly used among millions of practitioners in science and technology worldwide. In the absence of similarly clear and generally accepted standards, ethics involves continuing development and promotion of multiple theoretical options, including ancient traditions in various versions, purist to reformed, as well as eclectic blends from diverse sources and newly created value claims. Simultaneously with the variety of constructive developments and their promotion, ethics undergoes continuing rigorous and critical cross-examinations that widen the appeal of moral skepticism. Both critical deconstruction and ambitious efforts at constructive and reconstructive development characterize contemporary ethical theory.

Further clouding the comparative picture with science, ethical thought is complicated by the inevitable tangle of experiential, emotional, historic, aesthetic, economic, political, religious, scientific, and other aspects of reflection that contribute to our ongoing search for the life we want to live. This is why moral vision, our way of orienting ourselves to life, the internalized framework through which we act, is so important yet so difficult to account for. There are a great many influences on us as we form our moral visions, some imposed on us by chance, some by the designs or intentions of parents, friends, and our communities, and some that we choose to pursue for ourselves, deliberately putting ourselves into situations to provoke reflection and growth. The resulting works in progress (for we are remodeling ourselves as we go) defy causal explanation despite the fact that we construct accounts for ourselves and for others as we attempt to understand, explain, and justify ourselves and our actions.

Although arguments and evidence play important roles in showing how our actions follow from or are consistent with our moral outlooks, we cannot provide necessary and sufficient conditions for our moral visions themselves, and if we offer arguments in defense of them, we cannot expect anyone to be compelled to accept our internalized moral framework as their conclusion. Moral thinking cannot be reduced to formal proof. As suggested above, moral thought involves vision, imagination, and aspirations to meaning beyond conventional discourse. Yet those glimmers of meaning demand expression, so we find nondiscursive articulate forms, be they visual, literary, musical, metaphoric, or merely a gesture, a glance, or some other effort to connect reflectively with those around us. So, although ethical theory, like scientific theory, goes through crises that provoke paradigm shifts, the complex personal nature of moral thought makes value framework shifts more difficult for individuals and for societies to negotiate because standards are less uniform, variables are more diverse, and vested interests are more difficult to control. As Hobbes put it 350 years ago, "the doctrine of right and wrong is perpetually disputed, both by the pen and the sword, whereas the doctrine of lines and figures is not so; because men care not, in that subject, what be truth, as a thing that crosses no man's ambition, profit or lust."[3] Hobbes goes on to say that were a principle of geometry contrary to the interests of those having dominion, that principle would be disputed or suppressed, even by burning all geometry books, if the interested party had such power. History seems largely to confirm his suspicion.

Perhaps the biggest challenge for moral thought today is presented by the tension between the pluralistic reality in which we find ourselves and the reluctance to embrace value pluralism among individuals and groups in conflict. Cross-cultural contact has never been more common, yet traditional value perspectives tend to reflect dogmatic insistence on their own values as absolute. This is manifest among individuals within communities as well as between groups across religious, cultural, and national boundaries. Occasionally, individuals or groups with very different values coexist peacefully, but persistent conflict is more usual, with dogmatic value collisions often leading to the use of force in efforts to settle matters, those with greater access to resources simply asserting whatever it takes to prevail while rationalizing the resort to force. The less powerful resent the seemingly arbitrary impositions of force from above, with the most resentful and least powerful among them often turning to violence in retaliation or to assert their position.

Internal social conflict in the United States over lawful abortion is a case in point. Most citizens accept the legal reality, hold and act on their personal values, and acknowledge that not everyone agrees. A few citizens with particularly strong convictions one way or the other organize and advocate their positions politically. And a tiny minority of those in opposition to legal abortion use violence against clinics and individuals involved in providing abortions. For these few, value pluralism is unthinkable concerning abortion.

On an international scale, Western European and North American cultural, economic, political, and military hegemony is understood by many to be global progress yet it is resented by many as well, and resisted as dogmatically and with as much rationalization by those on whom it is imposed as it is celebrated by dominant leadership. For the most part, people, and nations, do not set out to do evil; most want to be moral, to choose lives that promise fulfillment, showing a measure of respect for the aspirations of others by adopting live-and-let-live practices. Yet we seem to bump into one another, individually and collectively, with increasing frequency, and the bumps between dogmatic adherents of conflicting values can be major collisions that result from aggressive actions meant to defend threatened ways of life. Where is morality in all of this? Must we resign ourselves to moral thought simply battling it out dogmatically, being rendered insignificant by relativism or skepticism, or being displaced by market values, by sheer power, or by violence?

Just when it seems that the Hobbesian war of each against all accurately describes human history we are reminded of the lives of Frederick Douglass, Jane Addams, Albert Schweitzer, Mohandas Gandhi, Martin Luther King, Jr., Nelson Mandela, and others on the global scene, or we recall a personal friend, relative, or stranger whose action, comment, or gesture touched us deeply enough for us to know that Hobbes does not explain all human behavior, that humans can and do act not only from narrow self-interest but from kindness, compassion, care, and service, even when these are counter to narrow self-interest. Just when moral skepticism or nihilism seem to be plausible and tempting, we see a film, speak with a friend, read a novel, reflect on a news broadcast, hear a concert, remember an experience, engage an image, or react to provocation by a teacher, and subsequently feel lifted by an idea, drawn into another's world and point of view, challenged to higher standards, inspired to live more fully, or recommitted to the hard work of understanding others. Such reflective encounters, large and small, are the stuff of moral thinking. We struggle to understand how they influence us and we struggle to explain and justify ourselves to ourselves and to others, but we do not doubt the significance of such influences on our moral lives.

Two of the major challenges to ethics, then, are resisting the subsumption of all values under market forces, on the one hand, and furthering value pluralism to minimize dogmatic value collisions, on the other. Recognizing a richer and more diverse array of legitimate influences on moral thinking while getting past the goal of modeling moral reasoning after textbook empirical science should help on both fronts. We can quit expecting ethical thought to be reducible to narrow notions of reason and evidence (and thus quit complaining when such reductions fail), and we can quit ignoring or apologizing for personal, historic, experiential, aesthetic and other influences on our moral thinking. This does not mean relaxing standards of accountability, but it does mean changing them. All of us have to explain and justify our actions to ourselves and to one another. Acknowledging that moral thought is not science, not reducible to formulas and proofs, not captured in necessary and sufficient conditions, but a complex and ongoing reflective process involving our whole orientation to life, who we are, what we have experienced, and what sort of life we aspire to, allows us to review disparate factors affecting our moral lives and decisions more honestly and accurately. Such a shift away from operating in the shadow of science stereotypes makes it easier to reassert moral concerns where they are being overwhelmed by market forces. If moral concerns cannot be dismissed as mere relative preferences, or explained away as dogmatic vestiges of cultural bias, or reduced to matters of economy and self-interest, then they may more legitimately assume a place beside scientific, economic, political and other interests and as a result may get taken as seriously as these others. Conceiving moral thought more broadly does not guarantee a resurgence of moral integrity over narrow, market-based self-interest, but it does help make it thinkable.

Minimizing dogmatic value collisions is another matter. One important step in this direction is expanding honest and reflective conversations between individuals with very different moral values, people who may live in the same community but are oriented to life through very different moral visions, who inhabit very different worlds, in Maria Lugones's sense of that notion. More conversations across such worlds will take us a long way toward deeper awareness not only of the diversity of value systems and perspectives, but also of the contingencies that contribute to our differences. It is much easier for us to relax our dogmatic insistence that everyone act out of deference to our values when we understand that we would have very different values ourselves had we been raised in different families, surroundings, cultures, and social systems. A simple recognition that others are attached to their ways of life every bit as much as we are to our own can reduce fear and defensiveness sufficiently to ease hostility and allow peaceful coexistence. This is a start. If we approach others expecting them to be like us, soon we are struck with how different they are; but if we approach others expecting diversity, we may find, or create, common ground. Reducing mistrust and fostering pluralistic conversations across differences is no easy task.

A few years ago, then President Clinton promoted his "One America" initiative to open a national conversation on the continuing racial divide in the United States. He created a high-level commission to study the problem and encouraged people to engage neighbors, coworkers, and community members across racial lines in open and honest conversations about race. A year later, the commission reported its recommendations, Congress was unwilling to commit the resources needed to implement them, there was no widespread surge in conversations across racial differences, and the initiative faded from the news. None of this was surprising. It is hard to imagine Americans engaging one another across racial lines about race given the persistence of ongoing de facto racial segregation, continuing inequality of opportunity, and governmental retreat from efforts to correct these problems. It is increasingly clear that longstanding official silence concerning the legacy of slavery in America is a major obstacle to moral progress.

With *The Debt: What America Owes to Blacks*, Randall Robinson confronts the collective denial that blocks the needed open and honest conversations, providing a window to a world shamefully unknown to most Americans. Robinson reminds us of the massive crime of slavery perpetrated by the citizens and government of the United States and of its continuing effect on descendants of slaves in the form of racism. He does so with a combination of personal experience and historical record that helps us imagine life from his perspective, helps us become at least partial insiders to his world, preparing a context in which citizens may begin facing up to all that slavery has brought upon the nation. Robinson's push to focus reflection on reparations for slavery more effectively stimulated conversation across racial lines, at least in the mass media, than did President Clinton's race initiative, in part because Robinson named and pointed to something widely known to have been too-long ignored, and in so doing, he captured much in the way of national moral attention. In contrast, Clinton's initiative amounted to just another political gesture. It is worth noting that the main difference between the two efforts to provoke moral conversation and reflection is largely aesthetic: what grabs and holds our interest, what draws us into another way of seeing, what challenges what we take for granted? The impact on furthering moral thinking is clear.

Unlike leaders of the United States following the end of legal slavery, leaders in postapartheid South Africa initiated a means to begin a process of reconciliation across their racial divide. South Africans had to come to terms with recreating themselves to make possible going forward as a nation in ways radically different from their past, often old enemies having to do so together. Some called for trials like those held in Nuremberg after World War II, trials to prosecute and punish crimes against humanity perpetrated by the former national government. Others, motivated by their own fears of prosecution or by a sense of the need to get beyond the past and to get on with building a new nation, called on victims to forgive and forget. Nelson Mandela's nonracialist government took a third route: remember and acknowledge.[4]

Prominent among the reasons for the new South Africa taking this third way was a clause in the Interim Constitution that had resulted from negotiations and compromise and that allowed for the peaceful transition from the National Party government to free majority elections: "amnesty shall be granted in respect of acts, omissions and offenses associated with political objectives and committed in the course of conflicts of the past."[5] Both the former government and the opposition parties needed this provision, and competing factions understood that national unity had to be emphasized over retaliation and revenge. The resulting Truth and Reconciliation Commission, focusing primarily on amnesty for honesty and on reparations, reflected the African communalist concept of *ubuntu*, compassion, recognition of the humanity of the other, and restorative justice, qualities personified by then President Mandela and by Truth and Reconciliation Commission Chair Desmond Tutu.[6]

While there is a long way to go, South Africa already has begun facing up to the worst offenses of its racist past. Meanwhile, the United States continues to avoid attempts at coming to terms with the worst of its racial history. My point in raising these cases here is not to address them, per se, but to highlight the significance of often neglected yet crucial aspects of moral thinking: political realities that force an issue to the forefront or allow neglect, moral vision of leadership in raising or denying problems, moral imagination in reaching past old analyses to new syntheses, acknowledgment of historical, personal, emotional, aesthetic, and cultural aspects of moral issues in resisting the reduction and subsumption of every concern to economic interests, recognizing dissonance between values and events with crises signaling breakdown of conventional morality, giving moral considerations high priority among our various concerns, and accepting the inevitability of nondiscursive forms of expression contributing to moral reflection, discussion, and understanding. All of these concerns and more constitute the complexities of addressing institutionalized racism, and the cases of American slavery and South African apartheid only underscore the shallowness and artificiality of reducing moral thought to a science of principles and rules.

This comparison of owning up to slavery with facing up to apartheid arose in the context of considering strategies for reducing dogmatic and absolutist imposition of values and expanding openness to value pluralism. Open and honest conversations across various value divides and more frequent reflections on pluralistic values seem to be steps in the right direction, and nondiscursive expressions can further their likelihood. Examples are all around us. The celebrated PBS series on race in America, "Eyes on the Prize," does more to engage moral reflection than hours of lectures and reams of editorials; the same can be said for many other television projects, films, photographs, stories, and plays. Aesthetic power grabs and holds viewers to actual and fictional depictions of torture, destruction, genocide, mass evacuations, mass demonstrations, as well as of acts of kindness, generosity, compassion, and service. Of course, aesthetic power also grabs and holds viewers with media manipulations of their feelings, thoughts, beliefs, and values. This is why we can catch ourselves sniveling through a tear-jerking drama or romance or cheering for Dirty Harry as he blows away the bad guy without due process of law. Aesthetic images can be very powerful. Often that power is used to reinforce traditional dogmatic imposition of values on others rather than to invite conversations and promote seeing things from new and different perspectives. It is easier and more common to use aesthetic and other powers to reinforce values already held than to open windows to other worlds, easier to encourage fears, defensiveness, dogmatism, and mistrust than to build trust, openness, and respect for pluralism.

This is an old story, one so old that it is the most plausible explanation for Socrates' execution in 399 BCE. The old stone cutter asked too many questions, exposed too many pretenders to wisdom, and embarrassed too many important public figures to be allowed to persist in looking beneath, behind, and beyond the manipulative claims he challenged. In a court of public opinion, use and abuse of aesthetic power may account for outcomes and alter the course of events. This is why Plato is so worried about artists in his *Republic*; after all, Socrates was executed for doing philosophy in democratic Athens, and persuaders convinced a majority of the jury to accept an image of Socrates as a corrupter of youth, teacher of false religion, and, with no little irony, maker of deceptive arguments. Reasons and evidence are important, but image, plus economics, politics, history, and emotions, all aided by aesthetic powers, may prevail when it comes to values and actions. Where is moral thinking in all of this?

As we saw above, Plato's antidote to manipulation is philosophy, critical reasoning. The point is that without critical thinking, without philosophy, we are more vulnerable to manipulations; but going so far as to ignore or deny the influences of economic, political, emotional, historical, personal, and aesthetic factors on the lives we aspire to live, expecting to reduce moral thinking to science, is to turn a complex, subtle, and multiple-aspect phenomenon into something one dimensional, which moral thought is not. Critical reasoning is necessary to moral thought, but it is not sufficient. It must be in dialogue with history, politics, economic realities, emotion, personal and cultural visions of life, aesthetic powers, and with those holding very different value perspectives; that is, it must be in dialogue with all that constitutes what we are. When such a deep and rich dialogue goes on, there are no guarantees that a final, once and for all, absolute and universal value or set of values will emerge. But the ongoing dialogue of multiple factors held accountable by critical reasoning is our best hope to expose pretenders to wisdom and to further understanding. At least it is the most reliable option yet devised, in part because it is self-critical and self-correcting.

Socratic wisdom involves admitting the limits of our knowledge, acknowledging that we have no monopoly on truth, accepting our knowledge as our best understanding at a given time and not insisting that it is final, absolute, universal, eternal, and immutable. After all, we are mere mortals, not gods; we are not infallible but are frequently mistaken; our experiences and perspectives are limited, not infinite, and so our values can only be partial at best. This means that we must be open to value pluralism out of simple self-honesty. Openness to value pluralism requires humble perception. Emphasizing the crucial role of Socratic wisdom, of critical thinking, of philosophy in its oldest and broadest form, in holding moral thought accountable has the added benefit of reminding ourselves that the goal of moral thinking is not a definitive criterion, final list of rules, ultimate formula, ideal set of necessary and sufficient conditions, or once and for all solution to the problem of the ages, the answer to the question "How are we to live?" The goal of moral thinking is to improve our practical wisdom, to strengthen our ability to make difficult judgments concerning the actions and practices constituting our lives. The goal of moral thinking is wisdom not knowledge, having good judgment not correct beliefs, living well not being right. Moral thinking connects all that we are with all that we aspire to be by refusing to be restricted by what is and has been, and by remaining open to what could be.

As complex and difficult as traditional ethical theory is, moral thinking turns out to be much more complex and even more difficult. Efforts to reduce moral thought to a single principle like the categorical imperative or the principle of utility, from which can be derived rules governing all human behavior, succeed only to the extent that they reduce moral thought to something less than it is, to something modeled narrowly after a limited conception of reason as it functions in stereotypical natural science. Traditional ethical theory captures an important part, but only a part, of the human struggle to answer the question "How are we to live?" A more complete answer comes from widening our concept of reason to admit all the disparate aspects constituting who we are, opening ourselves to consider our moral visions and how we came to them, and risking engagement of moral worlds unlike our own. Widening what counts as reason in ethics involves pluralism both in embracing diverse influences on moral thought and in acknowledging the possibility of multiple correct answers to moral questions. It does not necessarily reject absolutism or relativism, but it does not accept being constrained by such a dichotomy either. Widening what counts as reason in ethics recognizes the pervasive and often profound aesthetic influences on our lives, from the power of metaphors to the significance of images, novels, poetry, drama, dance, myth, music, and other nondiscursive articulate forms of expression. Recognizing moral thinking to be inclusive rather than exclusive—of lived experience, emotion, a wide array of perspectives from disparate cultures, whatever contributes to our reflections on how to live—opens moral thinkers to others, widening the possibility for complex, rich, and diverse conversations which, in turn, deepen our consideration of moral issues and options, and increase the likelihood of mutual understanding.

Traditional ethical theory has become too narrow, too technical, and too far removed from the stuff of moral thinking: experience, emotion, nondiscursive meaning, moral history, and the personal and communal relationships that make us who we are. The academic pursuit of the criterion for goodness has carried many to heights of dazzling intellectual and linguistic precision but may leave behind the very human struggle over how we are to live. I do not pretend to solve the problem by offering a better criterion or even a better method. Rather, I am only trying to help widen the scope moral theory by underscoring the diverse array of influences on genuine moral thinking as it goes on routinely among ordinary people. Rethinking ethics as a much richer enterprise than it has become in the last fifty years and opening more inclusive, diverse, and pluralistic conversations about how we ought to live should, at the very least, contribute to reducing and softening value collisions. Perhaps such conversations will help produce not criteria or rules, but guidance, good judgment, and practical wisdom reflective of the ongoing human struggle concerning how we are to live.

Moral thinking, it turns out, is an open-ended process involving ongoing interactions within and among individuals and groups, where disparate value frameworks, practices, and explanations stand in continuing review of one another. How could we imagine such a process collapsing into a criterion, principle, or set of rules fit for every human situation? Rather than settle the problem of the ages by determining how humans are to live, moral thinking refines good judgment using wisdom of the past, creative insight, and imagination to guide us into our individual and collective futures. Moral thinking cannot stop with any theorist or theory. It goes on in the conversations, practices, explanations, and imaginations of succeeding generations of reflective human beings.

NOTES

1. King, Martin Luther, Jr., *Why We Can't Wait* (New York: New American Library, 1963), 101.

2. Kuhn, Thomas, *The Structure of Scientific Revolutions* (Chicago: The University of Chicago Press, 1962, 1970), 64.

3. Hobbes, Thomas, *Leviathan* (1651), ed. Michael Oakeshott (Oxford, UK: Basil Blackwell), 68.

4. Conversation with South African Methodist Bishop Peter Storey, St. Paul, Minnesota, January 29, 1997.

5. Ash, Timothy Garton, "True Confessions," *The New York Review of Books*, Vol. XLIV, No. 12 (July 17, 1997), 33.

6. Ash, "True Confessions," 33

Afterword

Diversity, Relativism, and Nonviolence

There is something paradoxical going on in discourse among cultures. While on the one hand, there is an unprecedented intensification of informational interaction among the different cultures of the world, there is, on the other hand, increasing skepticism regarding the very foundation of such discourse; namely, the possibility of universal cannons of thought and action.

—Kwasi Wiredu

Our contemporary Western perspective has been characterized by increasing recognition of a wide variety of social, political, religious, and moral values — Western as well as non-Western — along with increasing acceptance of their legitimacy. Articles, books, and courses trumpet diversity, multiculturalism, and pluralism. We are urged to acknowledge and appreciate the meaning and importance of values very different from and sometimes in direct conflict with the predominant values of our own traditions. Moral collisions abound.

Historically, philosophers have considered arguments designed to justify certain values as universal, but during the last half of the twentieth century, value relativism gained adherents, value foundationalism was put on the defensive, and thinkers asserting any particular values to be universal became increasingly rare. In earlier chapters, I have reviewed important critical objections to the current state of ethical theory, including those of Alasdair MacIntyre in *After Virtue* and Richard Rorty in *Contingency, Irony, and Solidarity*. This changing intellectual climate or context of discussion makes it difficult for anyone to argue for the universality of any particular value, in part due to the diversity of values and their alleged equal legitimacy, and in part due to a common feeling, motivated to some degree by a kind of "self-critical recoiling from the earlier intellectual self-aggrandizement of the

103

West,"[1] that we are dogmatic, insensitive, or unenlightened should we propose any value to be somehow above or beyond those of egalitarian pluralism.

Meanwhile, paralleling the growth in recognition and acceptance of a plurality and a diversity of values, violence is increasing steadily on personal, social, and international levels. Perhaps the increase in violence is in some way related to the newfound acceptance of a diversity of values since every value is as good as every other on some readings of relativism, so violence has as much value as anything else. Perhaps recognition of diverse values inspires some to persist in dogmatically imposing their values onto those they take to be value mistaken, people with different values, with whom they come into contact. Or perhaps violence and awareness of value diversity are unrelated, increases in the rates of each coincidental with those of the other. In any event, all of this leads to the notion that the opening years of the twenty-first century have the distinction of being what may be both the most violent as well as the most enlightened of periods. I am not going to present reasons and evidence in support of this suggestion here; you will be spared citation of comparative data on levels of enlightenment as well as data on carnage by century. Rather, the focus here will be to extend the view of moral thinking explored above by applying it to the question of moral universality. In this extension and application of ideas developed above, I defend nonviolence as a good candidate for value universality despite, and, in a way, due to difficulties presented by the increasing prevalence of relativism. The argument involves an integration of discursive reasoning, aesthetic appeal, and pluralistic considerations, moral thinking admittedly at the edge of conventional academic philosophy.

There is a profoundly difficult philosophical issue here, one concerning perspective, context, and the legitimacy of value judgments across cultures. It is a problem that has plagued theorists throughout history and that is increasingly problematic with the passage of time and growing cross-cultural interactions. How can anyone presume to issue a value judgment that would hold despite widely different environmental, historical, religious, political, economic, and cultural contexts?

It is fairly easy to sketch the predominant conventional philosophic moves to address this problem. One position defends a notion of universal values, values true across cultural, historical, and other boundaries. This view has some dogmatic adherents—those who assert their own values as absolute and declare any values at odds with theirs to be wrong. But one need not be a dogmatist to defend value universals; value truths are considered by some to be analogous to scientific truths, steady progress being made through collaborative work. We may not yet have the final word on universal values—just as science is incomplete—but history reveals ever clearer moral truths, or so this position would maintain.

A second position, increasingly common in academic circles, is to deny value universality and accept value relativity across cultures. Again, there may be dogmatic adherents insisting that values cannot be said to be true at all, except insofar as one can report that certain individuals indeed hold them. Softer forms of value relativism may consider values true within their specific contexts, but deny meaning to values across contextual boundaries. In this view, values have meaning for members of a community, but otherwise they are meaningless.

Various positions between universality and relativism have been put forward, and critics typically attempt reducing them to one or the other of these two views. Projects in defense of universality often suggest increasingly abstract principles in efforts to identify like values from various cultures and embrace them under broad principles. Comprehensiveness of such efforts tends to such abstraction that critical challenges are grounded in charging that such broad principles are virtually empty of content. Projects in defense of relativism focus on the diversity of concrete values, often with particular attention to their incompatibility across cultures. Critics of this approach sometimes dismiss incompatibilities as differences among social mores rather than among crucial values and reemphasize value similarities across cultures.

I cannot pretend to resolve the ancient philosophical quarrel between relativism and universality in what follows. I don't even try to choose between these views. Rather, I attempt mediating the dispute by proposing a candidate for universality that itself reflects and rests on acknowledging diversity. Diversity considerations often are cited as grounds for skepticism about value universality, and value universality is usually taken to be in tension with value pluralism. I want to entertain the notion that these seeming incompatibles may, in fact, be quite compatible. Inspired by pluralism, I want to explore the idea that nonviolence may be a diversity candidate for value universality. For the sake of clarity, the scope here is limited to large-scale group or state violence, although there are important implications for interpersonal violence as well.

Etymologically, violence is derived from a Latin word meaning "vehemence," which itself derives from Latin words meaning "to carry force." So, violence literally means "intense force." It shares its etymology with "violate," which means "injury." Violence refers to both extreme force, as in a violent earthquake or storm, and to forced injury, as in rape, terrorism, or war.[2] By nonviolence I mean both an unwillingness—or at least a strong reluctance—to use violence to achieve goals *and* a disposition to use peaceful means to accomplish objectives, means compatible with ends sought. Nonviolence has a negative aspect—it stands against overt and covert uses of coercive force that violate—and a positive one—it involves cooperation, collaboration, and agreement-building as valued components of genuine peace. Here, genuine peace is understood as consisting not only of an absence of overt violence but also a presence of social order arising by the uncoerced choices and practices of societal members. Peace that is merely negative, orderly by force imposed onto group members from outside the group, is not the genuine peace we are trying to build. Given this notion of nonviolence, we can turn to how it may ease tensions between relativism and universality.

In any given instance of its use, perpetrators of state-sponsored or group violence are expected to justify their actions. According to conventional morality, where violence is justifiable, it somehow contributes to righting a wrong, establishes a just order where it was missing, creates peace where it was absent. Justifications rest on the presumption that, all things being equal, violence is morally wrong. Violence is not valued for itself but is valued, if at all, as a means to some other end. So, whether violence is justified or not in any particular case rests on knowledge. Perpetrators of violence have to be justified in their belief that the violence they engage in is allowed in the given case in order for their violent acts to be morally warranted. Without such knowledge, their violence would be immoral rather than justified, since violence is morally condemned in all but exceptional circumstances, namely, it is warranted only as a necessary response to prior aggressive violence. Violence is presumptively wrong, so wrong that only aggressive violence warrants further violence, at least according to conventional wisdom.[3]

One might challenge the presumption that violence is wrong on extreme relativist grounds: every value is as good as every other; violence and nonviolence are thus equally warranted or unwarranted. If one thinks an act of violence is justified, then it is, since each of us is "the measure of all things," in classical Protagorean terms. But this objection neglects the context within which considerations of morality and violence occur. As Michael Walzer has observed, "one of the things most of us want, even in war, is to act *or to seem to act* morally."[4] I take this judgment to reflect accurately the prevailing attitude or dominant outlook on violence and morality: publically, across cultures and despite widely varied religious, political, historic, economic, and cultural perspectives, violence is condemned morally and is accepted only where morally excusing conditions are satisfied. To underscore the general condemnation of violence, notice that when violence *is* advocated, the rationale always alleges violence that must be countered; that is, violence is so wrong that it is the only crime sufficient to warrant a violent response. My point in stressing this is to suggest that wanting to *seem* to act morally carries the burden of moral justification as well as wanting to act morally, at least when it comes to public acts, and especially when it comes to large-scale, international acts of violence. Both the perceived need to *seem* to act morally and the authentic commitment to act morally reflect a universal presumption that violence is wrong and result in condemnations of violence and in moral arguments to excuse violence in response to violence. Given the accuracy of this description of our context, the burden of justification rests squarely on those who would act violently.

We might wonder why the empirical conditions are as they are. Is the prima facie moral condemnation of violence merely coincidental to various cultures? That is, might it be a contingent fact that violence is condemned across cultures? Or does this prima facie moral condemnation of violence reflect a deep natural moral law? Is it consequent to particular environmental factors, derived from a common moral sense reflecting a common human nature? Or is it simply a consistent but relative consensus across cultures? Does it matter which, if any, of these accounts settles the matter? Whatever the explanation, the prima facie condemnation of violence characterizes something akin to moral universality. In an important sense, the de facto moral universality of nonviolence is more significant than the absence of a definitive explanatory account. Regarding public and especially large-scale and international acts, the presumption of the moral wrong of violence is certainly as close as the diversity of nations and disparate cultures gets to value universality. At the same time, I recognize the fact that, despite widespread condemnation of violence, nations and groups frequently practice and excuse violence as well. It is sometimes said that a culture's real values are reflected not in their value pronouncements but in their behaviors. Perhaps the crux of the matter is in how these two are related and particularly in how espoused values are used to explain and justify actions, since the persistent and widespread moral condemnation of violence is as common as violence itself. Clearly, violence is generally condemned morally, accepted only when excusing conditions have been satisfied, or, more accurately, when those employing violence claim that excusing conditions have been met.

Conventional standards for the knowledge in question that is supposed to warrant violence seem not to demand absolute certainty, but a fairly high likelihood of success at righting wrongs seems necessary to justify violence. Pinning down the exact degree of likelihood is not at issue here, but it is clear that the justificatory burden gets heavier proportionate to the scale of violence contemplated. A righteous imposition of violence surely involves claiming violence to be necessary in the case in question. Presumably, violence is thought to be required in defense of something taken to be more valuable than that which is sacrificed through the use of violence, for violence always involves sacrifice. And, it is important to add, justifiable violence requires the stipulation that nonviolence is thought to be unlikely to prevail in the case in question.

Increasing awareness of the diversity and variety of values tends to undermine the knowledge required to justify violence because it erodes confidence that any one thing should be valued over others or that one value rightly predominates over others. In this way, respect for diversity erodes the confidence those attempting to justify violence need to make their case. So, increasing respect for diversity should lead to increasing respect for nonviolence. Put another way, the appreciation for value relativism prompted by respect for diversity leads to appreciation for nonviolence as a possible value universal.

It may seem paradoxical that respect for diversity fosters appreciation of relativism, thereby undercutting the absolutism needed to warrant violence and consequently resulting in nonviolence as a potential universal value. But there is no contradiction here. Respect for diversity ultimately entails respect for nonviolence because violence must bear the burden of proof, and respect for diversity increases the burden. We cannot act in virtue of what we do not know unless we are to be irresponsible. As Gandhi puts it, the use of violence is excluded because we are not capable of knowing absolutely[5;] without sufficient knowledge we cannot justify acts, especially those that cannot be undone. As Gandhi sees it, it is wrong to cause others to suffer for what may be our mistakes. Even if we weaken the knowledge requirements from Gandhi's absolute standard to something akin to the standards of scientific knowledge, still, appreciation of diversity fosters considerations of value relativism that inevitably increase skepticism over any particular attempt to excuse violence. So, not knowing (about results that allegedly will justify a resort to violence) leads to a sort of knowing (about the moral preference for nonviolence). Here, I am defending what I have called epistemological or fallibility pacifism: "we simply cannot know relevant factors with sufficient confidence to warrant irrevocable violent actions between nations."[6]

If it is paradoxical that respect for diversity fosters appreciation for relativism thereby undercutting the knowledge needed to warrant violence, it is not unlike Socrates' knowing that he does not know, an epistemologically respectable position in which to be. Interestingly, when it comes to values, Socrates cites his *daimon*, or inner voice, that never tells him what to do but always dissuades him from unjustifiable acts.[7] This has an affinity to the Socratic expressions of nonviolence in the *Crito* that Gregory Vlastos has so ably explicated.[8] While traditional interpretations have Socrates adopting "we should never return evil for evil" only for the sake of the argument, Vlastos sites this as an early challenge to the dominant law of retaliation still prevalent in the Western value tradition. The common sense principle is something like "when in doubt, do not act in ways irretrievable."

The broad presumption that violence is wrong puts defenders of violence in a logically awkward—even contradictory—position when they are involved in attempts to excuse violence. Justifications for violence are always built upon opposition to violence and violation: because violence is wrong, it is argued, violence must be used to put an end to it. This is just the sort of double-think that must be exposed. If violence is a crime, as those justifying violence claim in their excusing arguments, then responding to violence with violence compounds the crime. Only sophisticated—or sophistical—thinkers could come up with this rationale. Ordinary good sense, checking the criterion that would justify violence against lived experience, understands that violence is a problem, not a solution. Experience seems to indicate that we choose violence when we fail to act on our ordinary good sense, when our best judgment is overridden by fear, anger, hatred, habit, or other impediments, when our moral reasoning is fragmented rather than integrated. Aesthetic judgment, direct and indirect as discussed above, seems to confirm the view that violence is prima facie wrong and only allowable if excusing conditions are satisfied. Moral thinking, in the form described above, requires a plurality of judgments fitting together compatibly and cohesively: reasoned argument, aesthetic sense, lived experience, emotional sense, all integrated and processed through a pluralistic moral framework resulting in a judgment not narrow, dogmatic, and insistent, but broad, respectful, reflective of difference, and tentative, the best we can do at that moment.

Defenders of nonviolence do not face the embarrassment of logical contradiction; their opposition to violence does not require its use, their moral objections need not be twisted and turned into excuses for allowing crime to resist or respond to crime. Defenders of nonviolence do face some logical tension however. As Jan Narveson has pointed out, pacifists—at least some— are in the odd position of being so opposed to violence that they are "not willing to lift a finger to keep it from going on" except, perhaps, by handing out leaflets.[9] Of course Narveson's objection, sarcasm aside, rests on confusing pacifism (literally "peace-making") with passivism ("suffering acceptance"), and on restricting the use of pacifism to only the most absolute adherents of the view. As empirical evidence amply demonstrates, the vast majority of pacifists are activists willing to do a great deal beyond leafleting to oppose violence as well as to support and to build community ordered from within by cooperation rather than from outside by dominating force.

Nonviolence can be defended based on traditional value frameworks as well. It is not difficult to argue from Kant's categorical imperative to arrive at a commitment to nonviolence. If one is to act out of respect for a principle that one can will to be a universal law, certainly nonviolence qualifies. Or, put in the practical formulation, if one is to act treating human beings as if they have value as ends in themselves and never to act in ways that treat people as mere means to other ends, surely nonviolence describes such behavior. Shifting to the other predominant value framework, it is not difficult to argue that the greatest good for the greatest number of beings in sentient creation would be served by nonviolence. History seems to confirm the claim. What is striking is how few Kantian deontologists and Millian utilitarians have thought their way to nonviolence. Perhaps Kant and Mill can be forgiven, considering their perspectives from within eighteenth- and nineteenth-century imperial Europe and taking into account that they had no experience of the work of Tolstoy, Gandhi, Addams, King, Mandela, and other twentieth-century peacemakers.

Of course, the argument to this point only makes the negative case for nonviolence by noting the incoherence of the case for violence. We admire Socrates, in part, because the negative case is always the easier one to make. But there is a positive side to nonviolence also—the commitment to social order arising from within society through the uncoerced choices and practices of community members. How is it that anyone embraces this value orientation, given the claims above that there are not reasons and evidence modeled after textbook science that constitute an argument sufficient to compel anyone to accept nonviolence, or any other moral vision, as their conclusion? A large part of the draw to nonviolence is experiential, not only from considering the moral giants such as Gandhi, Addams, King, and Mandela, but also from reflecting on personal experience both of violence and of nonviolence. Such considerations take us immediately to the aesthetic pull of nonviolence, the simple value preference we sense in our own lives as we reflect on the sheer attraction of uncoerced cooperative social order as compared with chafing under the imposition of coercive ordering which originates and comes at us from outside our control, will, or wishes. Yes, there are aesthetic aspects to violence as well; it gets and holds our attention and leaves its mark on our behavior. Still, given the option, who would choose not to choose, who would will to be coerced, who would abdicate self-control for forced-control by someone from outside us? Fear, anger, desire, habit, any disintegrated part of genuine moral thinking, can take us beyond our self-control, leaving us feeling compelled to take up violence as a means to some ulterior end. Yet, given a choice between order imposed by force and threat from outside or order arising from within by cooperation, we prefer the latter, nonviolence.

By way of our best moral thinking we choose nonviolence for ourselves, for the ordering of our own lives, often not realizing that it is peace we are making. Yet we sometimes forget that others, even very different others, have their preferences for nonviolence also. Fear or anger or an itch for revenge or a sense of helplessness or some combination of these and other influences can disintegrate our moral thinking and lead us to resort to violence. This is where diversity, relativism, and pluralism are helpful; they are constant reminders that we are mere mortals with limited perspectives in need of the viewpoints and experiences of others to check and enlarge our views past their otherwise partial glimpses. Nonviolence interrupts and exposes the centuries-old dogmatic absolutism that imposes itself above others and enforces its imposition coercively. Nonviolence helps us see that might can only establish might. Nonetheless, nonviolence cannot embrace a thoroughgoing relativism because strict relativism makes all values arbitrary. The recognition of difference prompted by increasing exposure to diverse people, cultures, and ideas can lead to questioning the allegedly absolute status of our own outlooks, sometimes resulting in defensive and offensive dogmatic insistence of our views as absolute, but also resulting at other times in toleration and respect for difference. Instead of having to choose between absolutism and relativism, those respecting difference can opt for pluralism, both avoiding a single, monolithic value dogma and avoiding giving up on understanding value differences. Pluralism leaves open the possibility of value universality while embracing the notion that conflicting values can have significant meaning in different contexts. Rather than choosing and defending a predominant value structure among the diverse many, rejecting the rest, and declaring all values equally arbitrary and meaningless, pluralism respects the contextual meanings of the many and focuses on mediating value collisions to the mutual benefit of conflicting parties.

Opting to mediate value disputes rather than choose among competing values reflects the positive side of nonviolence, constructing community and building relationships among and between various cultural, ethnic, religious, national, and racial groups. This is the ongoing work of those committed to respecting and celebrating diversity and nonviolence. If there is any truth to this approach to moral thinking, then the broad value presumptions of the current global situation provide a basis for movement away from dogmatic absolutism, confrontation, and legitimizing violence and toward pluralism, mutual understanding, and ever-widening acceptance of nonviolence. After all, violence cannot create peace. At best, violence can impose force sufficient to halt other violence, thereby providing negative peace for as long as the force remains in place. Events in eastern Europe during the past fifteen years make this point evident. Only nonviolence can create and sustain the conditions all of us enjoy to varying degrees, in different contexts, at several levels of scale, personal, familial, among colleagues, neighbors, and community members, within and between nations. That is, only nonviolence can create and sustain the cooperative and collaborative activity characteristic of genuine (positive) peace. Unfortunately, most of the time many of us take such conditions for granted and fail to understand that it is genuine peace we are making when our lives are constituted by uncoerced and mutually sustaining interactions.

It remains important to critique the inconsistencies of arguments supporting violence and to provoke wider recognition of the existence and necessity of nonviolence around us. Increasing awareness of and respect for diversity in all its forms and the attendant skepticism regarding absolute values provide an ironic support for nonviolence as a value beyond dogmatic absolutism and thoroughgoing relativism. This relationship, in turn, provides some basis to hope for a global future with less carnage, more understanding, and even building genuine peace across traditional divisions. What is needed, of course, is a dominant value paradigm shift, from taking violence for granted as the way to resolve value differences to taking nonviolence for granted, and consequently working out differences peacefully. What is needed is any integrated combination of argumentative, experiential, aesthetic, and imaginative influences that will lead us, in the words of Martin Luther King, Jr., to "the day when violence toward another human being must become as abhorrent as eating another's flesh."[10]

NOTES

1. Wiredu, Kwasi, *Cultural Universals and Particulars: An African Perspective* (Bloomington: Indiana University Press, 1996), 1.

2. See Holmes, Robert, "Violence and the Perspective of Morality," chapter 1 in *On War and Morality* (Princeton, NJ: Princeton University Press, 1989), 19–49.

3. See Walzer, Michael, *Just and Unjust Wars* (New York: Basic Books, 1977), 58–63.

4. Walzer, *Just and Unjust Wars*, 51, emphasis added.

5. Gandhi, Mohandas K., *Nonviolent Resistance*, ed. Bharatan Kumarappa (New York: Schocken Books, 1951), 3.

6. Cady, Duane L., *From Warism to Pacifism: A Moral Continuum* (Philadelphia: Temple University Press, 1989), 64.

7. Plato, *Apology*, 31d.

8. Vlastos, Gregory, *Socrates: Ironist and Moral Philosopher* (Ithaca, NY: Cornell University Press, 1991), 179–99.

9. Narveson, Jan, "Pacifism: A Philosophical Analysis," *Ethics* Vol. 75, No. 4 (July 1965), reprinted in *War and Morality*, ed. Richard Wasserstrom (Belmont, CA: Wadsworth, 1970), 71.

10. King, Martin Luther, Jr., *Why We Can't Wait* (New York: New American Library, 1963, 1964), 152.

Index

About the Author

DUANE L. CADY earned his A.M. and Ph.D. at Brown University and is professor of philosophy at Hamline University. He is author of *From Warism to Pacifism: A Moral Continuum* (1989), coauthor of *Humanitarian Intervention* (Rowman & Littlefield 1996), and coeditor of three anthologies. His teaching and research interests are in history of philosophy, ethics, aesthetics, nonviolence, development, and pluralistic critiques of traditional philosophy.